T0209289

# DO YOU HAVE TO TAKE SHOWERS IN HEAVEN?

AND OTHER KID QUESTIONS ABOUT OUR FOREVER HOME WITH GOD

## LINDSEY HILTY

WESTBOW
PRESS®
A DIVISION OF THOMAS NELSON
& ZONDERVAN

WestBow Press books may be ordered through booksellers or by contacting:

WestBow Press
A Division of Thomas Nelson & Zondervan
1663 Liberty Drive
Bloomington, IN 47403
www.westbowpress.com
844-714-3454

Scripture quotations taken from the New Living Translation, copyright ©1996, 2004, 2015 by Tyndale House Foundation. Used by permission of Tyndale House Publishers, a Division of Tyndale House Ministries, Carol Stream, Illinois 60188. All rights reserved.

Scripture quotations marked (NIV) are taken from the New International Version® NIV® Copyright© 1973 1978 1984 2011 by Biblica, Inc. TM. Used by permission. All rights reserved worldwide.

ISBN: 978-1-6642-8949-9 (sc)
ISBN: 978-1-6642-8950-5 (hc)
ISBN: 978-1-6642-8948-2 (e)

Library of Congress Control Number: 2023900845

Print information available on the last page.

WestBow Press rev. date: 01/24/2023

To my Sunday school kids: thank you for your fabulous questions about heaven. Your enthusiasm for Jesus is contagious! Thank you also to Eagan Ellis and all my young friends who created illustrations for this book. Your artistic talents far surpass mine. To friends and family who helped me edit this book and encouraged me along the way, I am so grateful! And, to my incredible husband, thank you for believing in me and supporting my writing goals.

# Contents

# 1

# What is Heaven?

Most people, even people who are not believers in Jesus, would say heaven is a place we go when we die. They might even imagine how they will get there and what it will be like. Some will rely on what they have been told or what they have seen on TV. Some might even say they traveled to heaven to see it and then came back to talk about it.

The truth is, we can imagine heaven all we want, but the only *true* source of information is the Bible. We need to open our Bibles to know what heaven is, how to get there, and what life there will be like. Because the Bible often describes heaven using colorful descriptions and storytelling language, people who love Jesus may understand some things differently. That's OK! This book is a guide to direct you to the answers you can find in your Bible. If anything is confusing, you should talk to trusted adults. Together, we will discover the awesomeness of our Creator and the incredible place He prepared just for us.

How do you feel when you think about heaven?

A. Scared or sad about death.
B. Excited to see someone I love.
C. Worried I might be bored or will miss home.
D. Curious if I am good enough to get in.
E. Don't think much about it at all—it is a long way off.

Thank goodness God created us to feel so many emotions, and we can praise Him that He is good, kind, creative, loving, trustworthy, and faithful! Because we know this about God, we can trust that heaven is an incredible place—better than any place we can imagine. Heaven is our true home because we will be there forever with Jesus!

## Can you get dirty in heaven? If you did, would you have to take a shower? Are there showers in heaven?

These are some of the great questions my Sunday school friends had one day when I asked them to tell me everything they were wondering about heaven. In this book, we will look for answers to those questions in the Bible. However, when we think about heaven and wonder about what it will be like, we do not have *all* the answers. For some of our wonderings we will just have to wait and see. It will be an amazing and delightful surprise! I love that we have such a creative, fun, and mysterious God. Just look at all the creatures He has made, and the beauty of His design. Isn't it fun to imagine the possibilities and dream about what else God has in store for us?

So why doesn't He give us *all* the details about our future home? Where are those important answers to questions like, "Will we be able to fly?" and "Will there be roller coasters?" God always has a reason for everything He does, and heaven will be beyond anything we can possibly imagine! As we look at some glimpses of heaven from the Bible, you will see how hard it is for our minds to grasp something for which we have no comparison.

Think of it this way: How would you describe a cell phone to the disciples?

"Well, you see, there is this plastic device you hold in your hand to call people."

"What is plastic?"

"Well, it is this hard material made from oil."

"You mean olive oil?"

"Never mind. The important thing is you can use a cell phone to talk to people anywhere in the world by using cell towers that ping off satellites in outer space."

"Cell towers? Satellites? Space?"

Get the picture? It would be hard to explain something as amazing as a cell phone to people from ancient civilizations who recorded their history on scrolls and who communicated through letters and messengers.

God gives us a glimpse without all the spoiler alerts. It means we sometimes must guess, dream a bit, or even use some logic. For example, God made us inventors, builders, artists, teachers, writers, and more. Because God creates us with unique personalities and gifts, we could jump to the conclusion that God will continue to encourage us to use our talents and abilities for His kingdom. These are essential to *who* we are.

**So, does that mean we can expect to have a Mario Kart tournament with Abraham and Moses?**

 With God, anything is possible. Why don't you suggest it next time you are saying your prayers? Who knows! The Bible does not tell us if we will get superpowers, or if we will be able to teleport. Those are valid questions, though, especially since in Acts 8:38–40 the Holy Spirit seemingly teleported a guy named Philip from one location to another. Check out the story!

We are not told whether we will have to brush our teeth, take a shower, or even wear deodorant in heaven, but if you did have to pay attention to personal hygiene, I think it is only fair to vote for the best option for getting clean.

> In heaven, if cleanliness is important, I will …
>
> A. Find the nearest bubble bath with unlimited hot water, a library of books, and a buffet of desserts within arm's reach.
> B. Look for an epic carwash-like shower where the hot water never runs out and there is no time limit.
> C. Waterslide into the nearest pool. Chlorine is as good as soap, right?
> D. All three choices sound "heavenly."

Isn't it so great that we can learn from scripture and have a bit of fun on this journey of discovery?

Your wonderings are important. If we do not address them in this book, you can ask your own trusted adults. Perhaps they can point you to places in the Bible where you can find answers. Never stop asking questions! God made you curious for a reason.

Speaking of questions, you will have plenty of places in this book to write your thoughts, take notes, and dig a bit deeper.

When you see this Bible icon, try looking up the verses in your own Bible to learn even more about God and His plan for you. You might also consider highlighting or underlining the words that stand out most to you so they are easier to find later. This is especially helpful when you discover a verse you like. Have fun and be curious.

# 2

## How Do You Get to Heaven? Do You Need a Ticket?

 I love that idea of a ticket to heaven! In a way, yes. You do need a ticket. Jesus is your ticket, and He has given us a map in His Word—the Bible.

We cannot reach heaven on our own. No airplane or rocket ship could get us there. No wishful thinking could teleport us there. You see, we are sinners. The wrong things we do, even the very small things, separate us from God. He is perfect. Even if we could find our way to heaven's gates, we cannot get in, no matter how good we have been, because we have a sin problem.

We need Jesus. He died on a cross to take the punishment we deserve for our sins. He rose from the dead three days later so we could spend forever with God as His children. We do not know all the wonderful details about *how* we will get to heaven's gates, but we have been given a few fun examples.

Elijah, a prophet of God, got an extra special ticket to heaven in a whirlwind while riding on a chariot of fire in 2 Kings 2:11. I think it is safe to assume that a chariot of fire is not a typical mode of transportation to heaven. Though, the Bible tells us our experience will be just as cool when Jesus returns.

For the Lord himself will come down from heaven with a commanding shout, with the voice of the archangel and with the trumpet call of God. First, the believers who have died will rise from their graves. Then, together with them, we who are still alive and remain on the earth will be caught up in the clouds to meet the Lord in the air. Then we will be with the Lord forever. (1 Thessalonians 4:16–17)

We do not know when this will happen. It could be today, or it could be years from now. We *do* know for certain that both the Christians who have already died, and those who are still alive when Jesus comes back for us, will join Him in the clouds in the blink of an eye. (To my friends who wished to fly in heaven, this might be your moment!)

Jesus will be both our ticket and our guide. He will show us the way. So, how do you know if you will be one of the people to join Jesus in heaven? It's simple.

Step 1: Ask God to forgive you for the wrong things you have done (your sins).

Step 2: Believe that Jesus is the son of God, and He willingly died on a cross for you.

Step 3: Commit to following Jesus and invite Him to be the leader of your life.

If you openly declare that Jesus is Lord and believe in your heart that God raised him from the dead, you will be saved. (Romans 10:9)

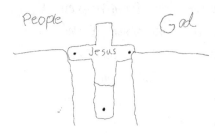

Have you ever seen a drawing like this? Once, someone drew a picture like this to explain why I needed Jesus. It made so much more sense in my brain to see it on paper. Maybe you can draw a picture like this next time you tell someone about how important Jesus is. You could explain it like this: Because of sin, we are separated from God. The penalty, or punishment, for sin is death. However, God loves us so much, He sent his son, Jesus, to die in our place. God made a way for us to be with Him forever. Jesus is like a bridge to heaven. By believing in Jesus, and asking Him to forgive your sins, you can live forever with Him.

God, You are loving and trustworthy, and You say I can be with you forever if I believe in You! Thanks for loving me so much that even when I was still a sinner, You died for me. But, You did not stay dead. You came back to life by rising from the dead, and You are preparing a place for me in heaven. Please forgive me for my sins and help me be more like You. I believe in You, and I trust You. I want You to be the leader of my life. Please guide my steps so I can serve You and follow Your plans. In Jesus's name I pray, Amen!

Check out John 3:16. What does the Bible say happens when you believe in Jesus? What do you think about this verse? Have you made that decision? Write about it below.

........................................................

........................................................

........................................................

........................................................

........................................................

........................................................

........................................................

........................................................

........................................................

........................................................

........................................................

........................................................

........................................................

........................................................

........................................................

........................................................

........................................................

........................................................

# 3

## Where Exactly is Heaven?

*"Oh, you can't get to heaven on roller–skates,*
*because you'll roll right by those pearly gates…"*

I used to love singing that silly song when I went to church camp.
Have you ever dreamed about finding a way to heaven? You are
not alone. The people of Babel attempted to build for themselves
a tower that reached to the heavens. Whether their focus was on
feeling awesome about themselves and their achievements, or
truly attempting to reach heaven, their effort and their downfall is
described in Chapter 11 from the book of Genesis—the first book
of the Bible.

*Babel by Abby, 10*

We have launched humans into outer space, so we know that
heaven has not been found in the "heavens," which can be another

word for sky. No tower would be big enough, or rocket powerful enough, to get us close to the pearly gates of heaven.

We know from the Bible that heaven is a place, but most importantly, it is the place where God lives. Don't forget that God the Father, Jesus, and the Holy Spirit are three Persons but one God. We will talk more about that later. The important thing to know is that Jesus is our "ticket" to heaven. We will not know the answer to where exactly heaven is until He takes us there one day.

There is a saying that home is where the heart is. Well, our heart is with God, and our home is with Him too. The Bible assures us that we have a home in heaven, and that home is being designed especially for us.

"Don't let your hearts be troubled. Trust in God, and trust also in me. There is more than enough room in my Father's home. If this were not so, would I have told you that I am going to prepare a place for you? When everything is ready, I will come and get you, so that you will always be with me where I am. And you know the way to where I am going."

"No, we don't know, Lord," Thomas said. "We have no idea where you are going, so how can we know the way?"

Jesus told him, "I am the way, the truth, and the life. No one can come to the Father except through me." (John 14:1–6)

What kind of place do you imagine God is preparing especially for you? What do you hope is inside your room? Write about it or draw it below.

# 4

## Is Heaven Just Like Earth?

This is a bit complicated, but let's dig deep to understand. Jesus has prepared a place for us, so when our bodies die, the rest of us (our souls—everything that makes us who we are) will join Him in heaven. Most people believe heaven exists outside of space and time. That means time in heaven is not the same as it is here, and we could not reach it even if we were the best explorers in the world. Heaven is a wonderful, safe place where we will find joy and peace. You can read more about this promise in John 14.

This place of heaven Jesus describes is going to be temporary. Our permanent home with Him will eventually be located on a new earth. When I first learned that news, I was a bit upset. What do you mean heaven is not in the sky somewhere like I always pictured it? It is difficult to adjust our thinking once we have something else in mind. That temporary place that God has prepared for us is not the end of His plan. He revealed this to John in Revelation 21:1. John saw a new heaven and a new earth, because the old heaven and old earth had disappeared.

Jesus is returning one day. It could happen at any time. We do not know the date or time. When Jesus appears in the sky, believers still alive will rise to meet Him in the clouds, according to 1 Thessalonians 4:17. That's not all, though. The bodies of those who have already died will be resurrected (raised). It will not matter where, or in what condition that body is in, because God can restore all things. This is a complicated topic that we could spend a lot of time studying, but the main idea is that God has promised us all resurrected bodies that will be perfect.

We have a supernatural and all-powerful God who can do anything. He does not give us all the answers to the how, where, or when, but we know *who* He is and *why* He wants to do this for us. He loves us.

So, when Jesus returns, (only God knows when that will be) all the people in heaven with Jesus will join those who are still alive here. There are a lot of events that will take place. The Bible talks about these events in Revelation, including a big battle where the angels will fight Satan and his demons. We already know the end of the story. God wins. Neither the timeline, nor the details about what will take place, are as important as the result—our forever home with God.

In a vision, God allowed an angel to give the disciple John a little tour of our future home. Here is what John saw.

> And I saw the holy city, the new Jerusalem, coming down from God out of heaven like a bride beautifully dressed for her husband. I heard a loud shout from the throne, saying "Look, God's home is now among his people! He will live with them, and they will be his people. God himself will be with them." (Revelation 21:2-3)

Jerusalem is an important city to God's people. It was the place the Israelites called home in the Promised Land after they left Egypt and wandered in the desert. It also was where they built a temple to God. However, they forgot about what God had done for them. They turned away from God and worshipped false gods. They disobeyed God, and the consequences of their sins resulted in them having to leave their home. Does that sound familiar? Remember Adam and Eve?

Jerusalem, the capital of Israel, is still an important place. After World War II, Israel was reestablished as a country, just as the Bible said it would be. However, if you ever read the news, there is *not* peace in Jerusalem. It is *not* the home God wanted for His people.

The new Jerusalem, that will come down from heaven, will be free from sin. It will be the place where God permanently lives among us. Can you imagine this perfect, sin-free earth? It will be recognizable, yet so different.

Adam and Eve's original home in the Garden of Eden did not include all the things that make life difficult, cause fear, or harm us. Mosquitoes did not bite, and bacteria did not cause illness.

---

Just for fun, put in order these annoying things about our broken home, with one being the worst and seven being the least bad.

_____ Cavities (Don't forget to floss, people!)

_____ Wasps (Ouch!)

_____ Jellyfish (Double ouch!)

_____ Viruses (Can you say, "pandemic?")

_____ Sunburn and frostbite (Can we call those opposites?)

_____ Clowns (fun fact: coulrophobia = fear of clowns.)

_____ Homework (Pop quiz, anyone?)

---

## How did this world get so bad, though?

Have you ever done something wrong? It can be awful to deal with consequences of bad choices or mistakes. For me, far worse than any punishment was knowing I had disappointed my parents. It left me feeling desperate to right a wrong—to make it up to my parents and gain forgiveness.

Adam and Eve had to leave their perfect home for one with death and destruction, not because that was what God wanted, but because that was the only option after they allowed sin into their lives. They could no longer live forever in heaven with a perfect and sinless God. The good news is God knew this would happen, and He did not leave humankind without hope. He had a plan to rescue them, and us, through Jesus. There is no need to earn God's forgiveness. He gives it freely. Sins are forgiven and we are loved just as much as we always were. Despite that forgiveness, though, we still must live with the consequences of sin.

> And to the man he said, "Since you listened to your wife and ate from the tree whose fruit I commanded you not to eat, the ground is cursed because of you. All your life you will struggle to scratch a living from it. It will grow thorns and thistles for you, though you will eat of its grains." (Genesis 3:17–18)

Have you ever pricked your finger on a thorn or gotten poked by a sharp thistle (those little thorn-covered spikey balls)? Those examples are just two things that cause us annoyance, pain, or struggles. There are so many more! In this passage, God is saying the ground would be full of thorns/thistles/weeds, but it also would be the same ground on which people would grow food like wheat and oats. God knew there would be hard things in this life, but there would be good things too. There would be consequences for sin, but God would continue to provide for our needs and one day defeat sin.

Notice the verse says God created those struggles *for you*. A great Bible teacher pointed that out to me once, and I have never forgotten it. God knew that this fallen world would not be our forever home, so He allowed these difficulties for our benefit. Imagine if this world had no bad things in it. We would never dream of a better place. We would not want to leave. We would be perfectly content here without those thorns and thistles making us uncomfortable.

Whenever you struggle, or face something difficult, you could think, "*Why me, God?*" or you could think, "*Heaven will be better. This is not my perfect forever home.*"

That perfect home He has prepared for us has no sickness, death, pain, sadness, or frustrations. He wants us to look forward to living there. Many people fear death, because they do not know about or believe the truth of what will happen to them after they die. Some people think this world is the best there is for them.

> Yet what we suffer now is nothing compared to the glory he will reveal to us later. For all creation is waiting eagerly for that future day when God will reveal who his children really are. Against its will, all creation was subjected to God's curse. But with eager hope, the creation looks forward to the day when it will join God's children in glorious freedom from death and decay. (Romans 8:18–21)

As a Christian you know where you are going and what you can look forward to experiencing. One day, God will call each of us home, and that day will be the perfect beginning to a perfect forever with God.

You do <u>not</u> have to be afraid of death. God defeated death. Our bodies may die here on this earth, but because of Jesus, we will live forever with God, first in the temporary place He has prepared just for you, and then permanently in our forever home on a new earth with all believers from all time.

Until then, God has given you a purpose. He wants you to worship Him and serve Him the best you can for as long as He has planned for you. You will have rotten days and hard feelings, like sadness or loneliness. No matter how many thorns and thistles you face, remember that God loves you and has a special plan <u>for you.</u> You matter, and He has given you gifts and abilities to do the jobs He has in mind for you. We need to keep our focus on sharing the good news that Jesus died for our sins, so anyone who believes can live forever in heaven as God's children.

---

List some of your gifts and abilities here. How are you using them for God?

1.

2.

3.

4.

5.

---

What are some hard things in your life right now that make you look forward to your future perfect home?

_____

_____

Check out Revelation 21:4. How do you feel about the promise in this verse? How does this help you understand our world now compared to heaven? If you have time, also look up John 16:33.

....................................................................

....................................................................

....................................................................

....................................................................

....................................................................

....................................................................

....................................................................

....................................................................

....................................................................

....................................................................

....................................................................

....................................................................

....................................................................

....................................................................

....................................................................

....................................................................

....................................................................

....................................................................

....................................................................

# 5

## What Does Heaven Look Like?

This was a popular question with my Sunday school class. They wanted to know the following:

1.  Is heaven rural or urban? (Meaning farm/country or city)
2.  Is heaven kind of like a huge building, or just a place with sky?
3.  How big is heaven?

While we can't know exactly what amazing sights await us in heaven, we can look to God's creation here, and to His word. There is a saying that a picture is worth a thousand words. Jesus revealed the picture of what heaven will be like to the disciple John through the Holy Spirit. John wrote the words Jesus told him to share with us so we too could know what to expect when Jesus returns, and what we can look forward to in heaven.

> So he took me in the Spirit to a great, high mountain, and he showed me the holy city, Jerusalem, descending out of heaven from God. It shone with the glory of God and sparkled like a precious stone—like jasper as clear as crystal. The city wall was broad and high, with twelve gates guarded by twelve angels. And the names of the twelve tribes of Israel were written on the gates. (Revelation 21:10–12)

What do we know so far?

1. There is a city (urban) that comes down from heaven.
2. There is a mountain (rural).
3. God is a creative God who loves to delight us with beauty and His creations.
4. We will have plenty of space to spread out in heaven, since a lot of us will be there.
5. Our new earth will be perfect, like what Adam and Eve experienced in the Garden of Eden.
6. There will be animals, since we know in the Garden of Eden, God told Adam to rule over the animals. Read Genesis 1 for a refresher.
7. God created plants for Adam and Eve and all the animals to eat. (Genesis 1:29–30)

> Based on what we now know, do *you* think heaven is rural, urban, or both?
>
> A. Urban
> B. Rural
> C. Both

What about the other questions: Is heaven a building or just open sky? How big is heaven? Glad you asked! God knew we would be curious about that, and can you believe He provided us with the answers in Revelation 21 starting in verse 15? You will need to look in your Bible to find out all the cool details, but here is a summary. John was given a tour of sorts by an angel, and this angel had a measuring rod of gold to measure the city gates and walls for John to observe and record what he saw. Here are some details he shared:

1. The city is a huge square, which you know means all sides are the same length.
2. The Bible also tells us the city is as wide as it is tall. Basically, it is big enough for us all!
3. The building materials are made of precious stones and gems.
4. The city is surrounded by nature as well as open sky.

If you have a book on rocks and minerals handy, or can look these up online, it is easier to picture this scene if you know what the rocks and gems look like. I used to have a rock collection, and I especially loved holding them in my hands and feeling the cold, smooth texture. I loved how they were polished and so shiny! The Bible says heaven is decorated with every kind of precious stone. Here is a list of the building materials and decorations described in this city:

- Jasper
- Sapphire
- Chalcedony
- Emerald
- Sardonyx
- Carnelian
- Chrysolite
- Beryl
- Topaz
- Chrysoprase

*Entering heaven's gates, by Lily, 9*

I am so glad God gave us a sneak peek into heaven, aren't you? What details has God revealed that you cannot wait to see in person? Do you have a favorite material from the list above?

........................................................................

........................................................................

........................................................................

........................................................................

........................................................................

........................................................................

........................................................................

........................................................................

........................................................................

........................................................................

........................................................................

........................................................................

........................................................................

........................................................................

........................................................................

........................................................................

........................................................................

........................................................................

# 6

## Is There Night and Day in Heaven?

This is a great question! Our days right now are divided into 24 hours and include daytime and nighttime. Sunlight makes plants grow and warms us. The dark of night can help us sleep well and provides us a view of our beautiful galaxy and the stars within it.

Still, I am not always a fan of the dark. When I was a kid, I had a big imagination and dreamed up all sorts of scary things to be afraid of in the dark. Thank goodness for night lights! I also dislike darkness because I prefer to be able to see where I am going! Can you relate?

Circle your favorite choice!

1. Would you rather walk barefoot across a floor covered with Legos, in the dark, in a room filled with spiders and spiderwebs ...

OR

2. Would you rather eat a mystery pizza in complete darkness knowing there is a chance your slice contains locusts, fish eggs, and the world's spiciest peppers?

Hmmm. I am not sure either sounds appealing! OK, back to business: light and dark! Have you ever heard Jesus referred to as the Light of the World?

Jesus spoke to the people once more and said, "I am the light of the world. If you follow me, you won't have to walk in darkness, because you will have the light that leads to life." (John 8:12)

Jesus is using an image here for us to think about good and evil. Darkness means all the evil of this world. When we follow Jesus, we are no longer living in that darkness. He gives us life forever with Him in heaven with no more darkness (evil). Light beats darkness. Good beats evil.

Remember how John received a revelation about heaven in a vision? Jesus sent an angel to give John a glimpse of the new Jerusalem that came down from heaven so John could share it with us in the book of Revelation.

Fun Fact: The Bible was written in a different language than ours. It had to be translated into English. Different Bible translations sometimes use a different word, or translators might write it in a slightly different style. Most Bible verses in this book are from the New Living Translation (NLT), because that is what we use in my Sunday school class. The New International Version (NIV) has slightly different wording from the NLT, but both are still God's true Word. You can look up the verses in different Bibles and see what I am talking about.

The city does not need the sun or the moon to shine on it, for the glory of God gives it light, and the Lamb is its lamp. The nations will walk by its light, and the kings of the earth will bring their splendor into it. On no day will its gates ever be shut, for there will be no night there. (Revelation 21:23 NIV)

Let's look at each part of this verse starting with how the glory of God gives light. If you look in the front of your Bible at the second book, Exodus, Chapter 34 describes how when Moses spent time in God's presence, Moses appeared "radiant." (See verses 33–35.)

Moses literally glowed! How cool is that? The glory of God—His presence—is brighter than the sun. The next part of the verse says the nations will walk by the light of God. Can you imagine? His radiance will fill every inch of the space around us. We will never have to stumble in the dark or trip over Legos. We will never be scared. There will be no more sin and evilness.

I love the last part of the verse about gates. Throughout history, we have created gates, or doors, to protect ourselves. In ancient times, the city guards would stand on the city walls and guard the gates to watch for danger coming during the day. At night, they shut the gates for added protection against attacks or troublemakers. Once we are given entrance into our forever home, we will never be shut out. We also will never have to fear that evil will enter our new home. It is a perfect and safe place.

And there will be no night there—no need for lamps or sun—for the Lord God will shine on them. And they will reign forever and ever. (Revelation 22:5)

 Check out 1 John 1:5. Don't forget, this is one of three letters John wrote and is near the back of your Bible. It is not the book of John in the Gospels (Matthew, Mark, Luke, and John).

God, thank you that You are light. Thank you that in You, there is no darkness. Sometimes I feel afraid, God, so please bring me comfort and protection. When I feel the warm sun on my face, God, help me to think of You and Your light. Thank you that one day I will see Your glory and live in Your presence. Amen!

Draw a picture of how you will look with a "radiant" face like Moses.

# 7

## Are There Roads in Heaven?

*The twelve gates were made of pearls—each gate from a single pearl! And the main street was pure gold, as clear as glass. (Revelation 21:21)*

There is at least one street in this new city God has described to us, and it is an important street! This one is made of pure gold. Interestingly, gold starts out dirty when you find it in nature. It must be purified, or have the dirt removed through a melting and refining process to get to what we see in jewelry. This street in heaven will not only be beautiful and valuable, but it will also be completely pure to the point of being as clear as glass! This description is a bit of a mystery, since gold is not clear, but I am excited to see what John was talking about. This description can also remind us that in heaven, we too will be purified. Our beauty and value will shine!

> Speaking of gold…
>
> 1. What do you call a piece of gold that is afraid of spiders?
> 2. What videogame do gold hunters like to play?
> Answers: 1. A Chicken Nugget! 2. Minecraft Source: www.funkidjokes.com

Get it? Gold comes in nuggets, and a person is sometimes called a "chicken" when they are afraid to do something. And, in the game

*Minecraft*, you mine for stuff. Aren't cheesy jokes the best? I crack myself up! Alright, let's get back to roads. As if this road was not spectacular enough, the angel we learned about in the previous question also showed John a crystal-clear river flowing from God's throne down the middle of the great street.

I love the picture that is forming in my brain, especially because I enjoy nature so much. God brought nature into the city!

When I visited Switzerland, flowing through the towns were rivers of clear icy blue water that had melted from mountain snow. It was so peaceful and powerful. I could have watched that water flow all day. There was just something about it that drew me in. The water feature in our future home will be completely clean and even more impressive than anything here on earth now!

> Then the angel showed me a river with the water of life, clear as crystal, flowing from the throne of God and of the Lamb. It flowed down the center of the main street. On each side of the river grew a tree of life, bearing twelve crops of fruit, with a fresh crop each month. The leaves were used for medicine to heal the nations. No longer will there be a curse upon anything. For the throne of God and of the Lamb will be there, and his servants will worship him. (Revelation 22:1–3)

Remember when Adam and Eve ate fruit from the tree of good and evil? The consequence was that sin and death entered the world. They, and every person who would be born after them, needed a cure. Jesus became that cure. The leaves of this tree of life symbolize medicine, because by defeating sin, God healed us. He saved us from death and gave us forever (eternal) life. Because Jesus took on the punishment for our sins, we can be reunited forever with God in His kingdom. We will be welcome to eat from this tree and remember what Jesus did for us on another tree (the cross).

I certainly am looking forward to tasting the sweet fruits of this tree! What is your favorite fruit? Think of a time you ate that fruit when it was perfectly sweet and ripened. Can you imagine how sweet the fruit from God's perfect tree of life will be?

A throne, a street paved with gold, a river flowing down the center with a fruitful tree of life on either side... What beautiful picture are you imagining? Draw it below!

Check out 1 John 1:9 *(Remember, this is the John in the back of the Bible, and not in the four Gospels).* Gold must be purified to get rid of the dirt and rock around it to make it beautiful. How are we purified?

What do you need to get rid of to become your most beautiful self?

_____

_____

_____

Thank you, God, for giving us a sneak peek of the most amazing place we can possibly imagine—our forever home with You. Thanks for showing us how beautiful it will be, and for answering our questions in Your true Word. Amen.

Lydia Torplee

# 8

## Is There a Wall Separating Heaven from Hell?

We now know *where* heaven will be—with God! But, what about the location of hell? My daughter and I were talking about her worries, and she wondered what would happen if Satan tried to sneak into heaven. Thankfully, that is not possible!

> Nothing evil will be allowed to enter, nor anyone who practices shameful idolatry and dishonesty—but only those whose names are written in the Lamb's Book of Life. (Revelation 21:27)

Pop Quiz!

### What is this Lamb's Book of Life that is so important to our entry to heaven?

Don't worry if you don't know the answer. We can find it together in God's true Word. Did you know that Jesus often is compared to a lamb? To find out why, we need to look back in the Old Testament.

God so loved the people He created, He wanted to be with them. However, sin separated them/us. To be able to dwell (or temporarily live) near the people, God instructed them to build a tabernacle—a church of sorts. God gave them a bunch of rules. Only the High Priest was allowed inside The Most Holy Place of the tabernacle, and he had to go through a complicated process to cleanse his sins before he could approach God. This High Priest would make animal sacrifices and offerings on behalf of God's people to serve as a substitution for the punishment they deserved for their sin.

No matter how often they made sacrifices and offerings, though, they still had a sin problem. God temporarily put this process into place knowing that one day He would offer His Son as a permanent solution.

Fast forward to the story of Moses in Exodus 11–13. The Israelites were told to kill (sacrifice) a lamb and place its blood over the doors of their homes to protect their first-born sons from death when God sent the final plague to Egypt to convince Pharaoh to free God's people from slavery. This was called Passover.

- Jesus is like that Passover lamb. His blood saves us.
- Jesus is our High Priest, making us forever right before God and making it possible for us to enter God's presence.
- The Bible tells us God will make his permanent home with us in our forever life with Him.

> So Christ has now become the High Priest over all the good things that have come. He has entered that greater, more perfect Tabernacle in heaven, which was not made by human hands and is not part of this created world. With his own blood—not the blood of goats and calves—he entered the Most Holy Place once for all time and secured our redemption forever. (Hebrews 9:11–12)

John the Baptist made sure people recognized the importance of Jesus. Look what he called Jesus in this verse.

> The next day John saw Jesus coming toward him and said, "Look! The Lamb of God who takes away the sin of the world! (John 1:29)

Remember the pop quiz question about the Lamb's Book of Life? To have your name written in this book means you understand the sacrifice Jesus made when He paid the penalty for your sin. Through Jesus, you receive God's righteousness (or goodness). In heaven, we will all have that permanently—no more sin. When you trust Him to be the leader of your life, your name will be written in the Lamb's Book of Life, and you can be certain of where you will spend forever. Satan never will be able to reach us in heaven.

**So, where does everyone else go if their name is not in God's book?**

This is one of the toughest things we face as Christians. Not everyone will go to heaven.

This truth is upsetting—very upsetting! I want everyone I love to go to heaven. I am sure you do too. That is why it is so important for us to share Jesus with others. He is the ticket to heaven! People who do not spend their forever with Jesus will go to a place of punishment without Him. It is called hell, and it is a real place.

 Check out John 10:1–21. You will notice we are referred to as the sheep, and Jesus is our Shepherd. What do you think Jesus means when He talks about a gate in this parable (story)? Underline your favorite parts of this chapter, and then write here why they are important to you.

# 9

## Where is Hell?

Right now, Satan is allowed to roam the earth. He is allowed to cause trouble and fool people, but there will come a time when God punishes Satan. Remember, by dying on the cross and rising from the dead, Jesus defeated sin. We are just waiting for God to finish what He started. Meanwhile, God is giving people time to turn to Him—to choose to love Him and accept His gift of salvation. When Jesus returns, He will act as judge. People will be out of time to choose. There will not be a scale of how good or bad someone has been. We all are sinners. None of us is good enough to tip that scale in our favor. Only Jesus can make us right before God.

The Bible tells us in Revelation 20:10 that Satan will be "thrown into the fiery lake of burning sulfur." He will never be able to leave hell.

The Bible talks about hell in Luke 16:19–31. Jesus tells about a beggar named Lazarus and a rich man who ignored Lazarus every day instead of helping him. Lazarus died and was taken to heaven where the Bible said he stood by Abraham's side. The other man went to hell where he was tormented. Hell is an awful place. The rich man looked up and saw Lazarus and Abraham far away. He asked for water and comfort but received none. He wanted to go back and warn his brothers so they would learn from his mistakes. Abraham told him that was not possible.

*"...and besides, there is a great chasm separating us. No one can cross over to you from here, and no one can cross over to us from there." (Luke 16:26)*

The rich man could not go back to warn his brothers. Once we die, we cannot go back and visit people or talk to them. This man was *down* in a place *away* from where his brothers lived. Most references to hell use words like down, down in the earth, or a pit. Just like with heaven, we can't point to the exact place.

We do know a few key things for certain.

1. Heaven and hell will be separate places, based on the Bible's assurance that heaven is with God. Only people who choose God will be with Him forever.
2. We also know that people can't cross from one to the other.
3. We know that Satan is defeated, and he won't be able to harm us in heaven.
4. Jesus clearly warns people about hell and asks us to accept the gift he is offering—to save us from it.

> Can you imagine struggling to make the choice if Jesus gave you these two options?
>
> Choice 1: Spend forever in heaven with God, who is light, love, peace, joy, and all good things.
>
> Choice 2: Spend life apart from God and all He offers us. In hell, there would be no love, no joy, no hope, and no peace.

The choice does not seem like it would be a hard one, yet Satan is good at telling lies! Satan is good at making people happy and comfortable in this life, so they are not concerned about their forever life without God.

What questions do you still have? This is one of those topics that might be helpful to discuss with your parents or Sunday school teacher. Let them know how you are feeling about heaven and hell. Talk to them about whether you have made the choice to follow, or not to follow Jesus. If you are still unsure about whether you want to follow Him, keep reading, and keep asking questions until you get the answers you need to trust Jesus.

Dear Heavenly Father, please help us to understand Your Word and Your Truth. You love us so much, and You want to be with us. Sometimes we face hard things. Sometimes the people we love turn away from You. Thank you that You understand and care about our feelings. The Bible tells us that Jesus wept, so we know that You understand our tears. You want us to live with You one day in our forever home, without sin, or sadness, or pain. Help us to remember that thorns and thistles are here *for us* so that we want to be with You forever. In Jesus's name we pray, amen!

# 10

## Are There Different Ways to Get to Heaven?

Did you know there are people who believe they are Christians, but they never truly understand the gift of salvation? I was one of those people. I often said my prayers, just in case God was listening, because I was worried that I would not be allowed into heaven. I believed in God, but I did not trust Jesus as my Savior. I did not know it was possible to be *certain* I would go to heaven, and most of what I knew about Christianity was from what I was told or what I imagined was true. I never picked up a Bible to read, because I had heard it was too difficult to understand it for myself.

I needed a relationship with Jesus. While eventually I wanted to go to church, read my Bible, and spend time with God; before I got to that point, I needed answers. I did not realize so many answers to my questions could be found in the Bible until a new friend in eighth grade showed me in God's Word where I could look up what I wanted to know. I loved being able to discover answers, but even after reading the words, I still struggled to accept God's plan.

"But there can't be just one way into heaven!" I insisted. "That is not fair! How could anyone believe God would send people to hell?"

I wrestled with this a lot! Eventually, I realized God was not sending people to hell. He was saving people from it. People have come up with all sorts of ideas about what life after death looks like. We do not need to imagine it, though. God already told us in the

Bible what awaits us. We just need to read it to know His plan for us. God will not force anyone to love Him. But, for those who do choose to love God, he offers a forever life free from sin and death.

I finally realized I needed God to fix my sin problem, and He did that by sending Jesus to die on a cross and rise from the dead three days later. Jesus himself told us there was no other way but through Him. The Bible reminds us of this truth repeatedly.

> For everyone has sinned; we all fall short of God's glorious standard. (Romans 3:23)

> There is salvation in no one else! God has given no other name under heaven by which we must be saved. (Acts. 4:12)

God heard me asking questions. He put people in my life to point me to answers in the Bible. God loves when we ask questions, and He gives us the resources and the wisdom we need to find and understand the answers.

> If you need wisdom, ask our generous God, and he will give it to you. He will not rebuke you for asking. (James 1:5)

God wants us to keep learning, keep asking, and keep growing. If you are not excited about going to church, that is OK. God is still working in your life as you figure things out. One day soon, I pray you will find the joy, peace, and love that comes from a friendship with Jesus. I pray you will see how amazing it is to be part of a church family of believers. Until then, keep digging, keep asking questions, and keep praying.

Check out Matthew 7:13–14. What does Jesus say about the path to Him? If you want an extra challenge, read 2 Peter 2:4–9 and find an adult to talk through these verses with you.

# 11

## Are There Different Heavens?

There are lots of ideas people imagine about heaven, depending on what they have been told, or what they have read or seen in places other than the Bible. There are people who believe there is a god, but they also think there are many paths to heaven. Some think if you are a good enough person, surely God will make an exception for you. Some might even say you can get into different levels of heaven—like the best people go to the best heaven, and somewhat good people get put in a place where they have a second chance to get into a better heaven.

The problem is that those ideas are *not* in the Bible. The Bible talks about the "heavens" in the book of Genesis when God created the heavens (the sky) and the earth, but that does not mean there is more than one heaven when we die. When Jesus talks about the place of heaven, He most often says it is the place where we will be with the Father. It is our forever home with God. There is only one God, so that means there can only be one heaven.

Everybody in God's family will be loved and accepted equally. There will not be better accommodations for people who were "good" compared to people who were "not as good." When God looks at our sin problem, He does not have a system of deciding which sins are worse than others. There is no sin scale weighing our actions. When we repent, (say we are sorry and do our best to stop doing wrong things) God forgives us all equally.

If there was another way, or more than one heaven, God would have told us. Remember, Jesus said in John 14:6 that He is the way to heaven, the truth, and the life. Nobody can be with God except through a relationship with Jesus. We can always trust what Jesus says.

> "Soon the world will no longer see me, but you will see me. Since I live, you also will live. When I am raised to life again, you will know that I am in my Father, and you are in me, and I am in you. Those who accept my commandments and obey them are the ones who love me. And because they love me, my Father will love them. And I will love them and reveal myself to each of them."
>
> Judas (not Judas Iscariot, but the other disciple with that name) said to him, "Lord, why are you going to reveal yourself only to us and not to the world at large?"
>
> Jesus replied, "All who love me will do what I say. My Father will love them, and we will come and make our home with each of them." (John 14:19–23.)

How is it that Jesus is in His Father and we are in Jesus? I think of it this way. We are part of God's family. God the Father, Jesus the Son, and the Holy Spirit are separate, yet still one God. We belong to our three-in-one God, and through Him, we are given life. The Holy Spirit lives in us. We can feel His presence and guidance. The Bible says we are a temple of the Holy Spirit. Have you ever held a parent's hand and felt safe? I feel safe knowing I am held close by God.

My Sunday school class recently studied a passage in John 15 that talks about us being connected to Jesus like a vine and branches. Apart from Him, we cannot grow "fruit" like love, joy, peace, patience, kindness, goodness, gentleness, faithfulness, and self-control. A tree branch not connected to a tree will die. It will not grow fruit. Just like a tree branch, we need to be part of Jesus to grow fruit and to have life forever with Him. Jesus will make us right or righteous, but only through His own rightness or righteousness.

If "with God" is where heaven is, then there is only one place where heaven is located because God tells us He is the only God. When we are in Him, we share in the power of the Holy Spirit, and we experience life everlasting.

Check out 2 Peter 3:9-10. Do you know someone who needs to hear about Jesus?

......................................................

......................................................

......................................................

......................................................

......................................................

......................................................

......................................................

......................................................

......................................................

......................................................

........................................................
........................................................
........................................................
........................................................
........................................................
........................................................
........................................................
........................................................
........................................................
........................................................
........................................................
........................................................
........................................................
........................................................
........................................................

Thank you, God, that we are given life through You. Thank you that where You are, we will be one day. It feels sad to think about our friends and family members who have not yet turned to You for love and forgiveness. Thank you that You have not given up on them, and You are patiently waiting for them to choose You. Please help me to be a source of love and truth, reflecting You in all my actions and words. In the name of Jesus I pray, Amen!

# 12

## Are There Plants and Animals in Heaven? What About Dinosaurs?

Yes, there will be plants and animals in heaven because God made them, and they existed in the Garden of Eden.

> So the Lord God formed from the ground all the wild animals and all the birds of the sky. He brought them to the man to see what he would call them, and the man chose a name for each one. (Genesis 2:19)

This garden was an unbroken place where there was no death. No animals would have needed to eat each other to live. They ate plants instead, according to Genesis 1:30. There was no fear. No matter how large the reptile, or how enormous the beast, everything in the garden was peaceful prior to sin. If God created it, then it was there. Then, everything changed.

> Then the Lord God said, "Look, the human beings have become like us, knowing both good and evil. What if they reach out, take fruit from the tree of life, and eat it. Then they will live forever." So the Lord God banished them from the Garden of Eden, and he sent Adam out to cultivate the ground from which he had been made. After sending them out, the Lord God stationed mighty cherubim to the east of the Garden of Eden. And he placed a flaming sword that flashed back and forth to guard the way to the tree of life. (Genesis 3:22–24)

God could not let Adam and Eve live forever in their sinful state, separated from Him. Death had entered the world. God told them they could farm the ground, and He provided for their needs for survival outside the garden. They, and all people, would face hardship, but He would never leave them. God still loved them. God wanted people to live forever with Him. To do that, God needed to defeat sin and death. The sacrifice Jesus made on the cross accomplished this. It is how we can get back to that unbroken life Adam and Eve had with God in the Garden of Eden.

### So, what about dinosaurs?

In Romans 8:21–22 it says all of creation looks forward to when things will be restored and there will be no more death and decay. God *could* restore any animal, extinct or otherwise. Will He, though?

This will be left for us to wonder...

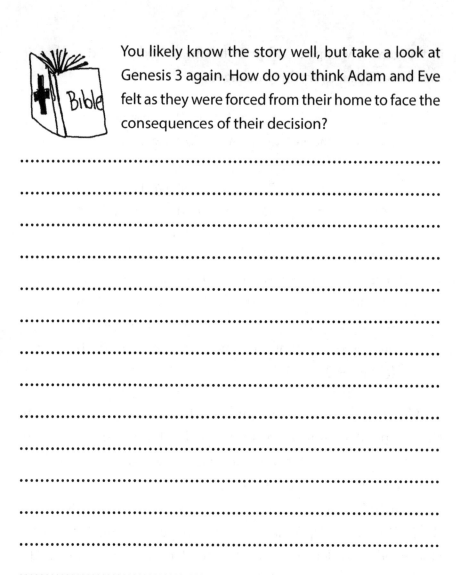

You likely know the story well, but take a look at Genesis 3 again. How do you think Adam and Eve felt as they were forced from their home to face the consequences of their decision?

....................................................................

....................................................................

....................................................................

....................................................................

....................................................................

....................................................................

....................................................................

....................................................................

....................................................................

....................................................................

....................................................................

....................................................................

....................................................................

....................................................................

....................................................................

....................................................................

....................................................................

# 13

## Do Our Pets Go to Heaven?

*Eliza, 10, and her pet dinosaur*

There is no clear answer that I can find for this question. People sure do love their pets. Pets bring them joy. They bring comfort. They become part of the family. The thing about animals, though, is they do not have souls like we do. They cannot choose to follow Jesus like we can. They were not promised a forever with God like we were. However, God can do all things, and He delights in bringing us joy. Animals existed in the Garden of Eden, and they will exist on our new earth as well.

The cow will graze near the bear. The cub and the calf will lie down together. The lion will eat hay like a cow. The baby will play safely near the hole of a cobra. Yes, a little child will put its hand in a nest of deadly snakes without harm. Nothing will hurt or destroy in all my holy mountain, for as the waters fill the sea, so the earth will be filled with people who know the Lord. (Isaiah 11:7-9)

There will be no death in heaven, even among animals. It is possible God has plans for your pets to join you. Or, He might have even greater surprises in store for you. I know a few friends who would not mind having a pet (vegetarian) T–Rex.

One of my Sunday school friends also asked me if animals will talk in heaven. This might be possible too. After all, God did allow an animal to talk to someone from the Bible. You are going to have to do a bit of extra reading to find out what happened!

 Read about an animal talking in Numbers 22:21–39! We have seen God do amazing things. If you could have any pet you could imagine in heaven, what would it be? If you could dream up a creature we don't yet have on our planet, what would it look like? Draw or write about it below.

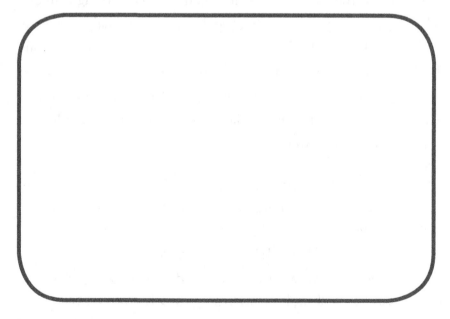

# 14

## Will There Be Any New Species in Heaven?

We have lots of amazing species in this world. Scientists think there still are creatures we have yet to discover. I imagine there will be incredible creatures in heaven.

One cool sight awaiting us is angels! Angels are not new species—they were created before us. However, we will be able to see and recognize them in heaven. It will be like Elisha's servant in 2 Kings 6 when God opened his eyes to see that an army of angels and fiery chariots had been standing with him all along. They far outnumbered the enemy troops there to do battle. We may not see them right now, but angels exist, and they are fighting on our behalf.

Angels are like us in some ways, but they are not the same as humans. The Bible has a lot to say about these created beings. Did you know Satan is a fallen angel? He tried to make himself as great as God, and for that, he and the angels that chose evil over good were kicked out of heaven. God will punish them, and they will one day spend forever in hell.

What else does the Bible say about angels?

1.  Angels are immortal beings. The ones who love God will live with us forever in heaven. Fallen angels on Satan's side will be punished and imprisoned in hell.

And they can no longer die, for they are like the angels. (Luke 20:36)

2. Angels worship God.

Then I looked and heard the voice of many angels, numbering thousands upon thousands, and ten thousand times ten thousand. They encircled the throne and the living creatures and the elders. In a loud voice they sang: "Worthy is the lamb, who was slain, to receive power and wealth and wisdom and strength and honor and glory and praise." (Revelation 5:11-12)

3. Angels have different responsibilities. Some came to bring announcements, like to Mary, Joseph, and the shepherds. Some are warriors. They protect us and will carry out God's judgment one day. Others serve us without us even knowing it!

Do not forget to entertain strangers, for by so doing some people have entertained angels without knowing it." (Hebrews 13:2)

4. Angels fight for us. Check out 2 Kings 6:15-17. Elisha's servant was scared they were outnumbered, but really, they were surrounded by angels ready to do battle.

5. Angels celebrate us. Did you know there is a celebration in heaven every time someone accepts Jesus as their Lord and Savior? That means they cheered for you if you made that decision.

"In the same way, I tell you, there is rejoicing in the presence of the angels of God over one sinner who repents." (Luke 15:10)

I don't know about you, but I am certainly excited to meet some of the angels who likely already know me! It comforts me to know there are angels in this world protecting me from harm, even when I cannot see them. If you ever feel scared, read Psalm 91! I especially like verse 11.

For he will order his angels to protect you wherever you go. (Psalm 91:11)

 Check out Isaiah 14:12–15 from the Old Testament, and Jude 1:6 which is the book right before the last book of the Bible. It tells us about what happens to Satan and his fallen angels, who are now demons.

Lord, thank you for providing angels to protect me. When I am scared, please help me to remember that I can command Satan to leave me alone because I belong to Jesus. Thank you also that one day in heaven, I will get to experience your creation in entirely new ways. Amen!

# 15

## When We Die, Do We Become Angels?

No. We will never be angels. Have you ever heard someone say, "Heaven got another angel" or that a person "got their wings" after dying? If you thought you would become an angel when you died, you are not alone. Many people believe this even though it is not in the Bible. Why is that?

If you hear something stated as fact, or repeated by several people, you might think it is in the Bible, or that it is true because you were told it was true. You might have even heard it from an adult in your life. That is why it is so important to read God's Word to discover truth. Otherwise, things can be confusing, even for adults.

We can think about it this way. God created cats and dogs. They are fabulous creatures. However, when we die, we will not become cats or dogs. We will remain human. It is the same thing with angels. God created angels. They are not an animal. They are not human. They are angels, and they live forever, glorifying, worshipping, and serving God. They are created heavenly beings.

Hebrews 1:14 says angels serve us.

Psalm 91:11 says angels protect us.

Hebrews 1 tells us that Jesus is Lord of all and superior to all angels. Remember that God, Jesus, and the Holy Spirit always have existed as one God, and God created all other beings on earth and in heaven. God created humans in His image.

Jesus, we thank you for bringing us Your Word. It can be confusing sometimes to figure out if what we hear is true, but it is so good to know the Bible is *always* true, and we can find answers there! Thank you for giving us curious minds to study, and for helping us understand when we are incorrect or misguided. Amen!

# 16

## Do Angels Really Have Wings?

This is a good question. We often see artwork depicting Jesus as a fair-skinned handsome man with wavy long hair. Yet, that is not how the Bible describes Jesus in the book of Isaiah, nor how Jewish men of that time and location would have appeared. Isaiah was a prophet, and he told of Jesus long before Jesus was even born.

*...There was nothing beautiful or majestic about his appearance, nothing to attract us to him. (Isaiah 53:2)*

We often see paintings of angels that look like cute little babies, or small humans with wings, but are these accurate? The Bible indicates otherwise.

The Bible describes different types of angels with different jobs and even different appearances. For example, in Hebrews 13:2 we are warned to be nice to strangers, because we never know when that stranger might be an angel. So, these angels must be able to look enough like people to be able to walk among us without us knowing they are angels!

Another angel, glowing with the glory of God, appeared to the shepherds in the field to announce the birth of Jesus, and the first words spoken were, "Fear not!" That angel must have looked fearsome or awe-inspiring.

God placed cherubs, or cherubim, as guards in front of the Garden of Eden. Before you picture a cute little baby, I should point out that Satan was a cherub before he was thrown out of heaven. This type of angel is powerful! In Exodus 25:20, God instructs the builders of his tabernacle, or temple, to make an Ark and to decorate its cover with cherubs spreading their wings above to protect it. God would not have instructed them to create this artwork in such a way if cherubs did not have wings!

So, to answer this question, we do know that at least some angels have wings. We know angels are beautiful creations of God, and there are different types of angels with different jobs to do. I imagine, just like us, angels will have unique appearances.

*by Ellie, 11*

 There are some impressive creations awaiting us in heaven. You can read about some of them on your own. Check out Ezekiel 1. It is a long chapter, but if you want a super cool image of heaven, it is worth reading. Remember the idea of trying to describe a

cell phone to the disciples? This is what Ezekiel is trying to do for all of us. How in the world does someone explain what he sees when everything is so far beyond his and our understanding? What do you think angels look like?

# 17

## Do Physics and Science Matter in Heaven—Like Gravity and Atomic Power? Is There Weather?

Let's start with gravity. It is likely safe to assume that gravity will exist in heaven, since we already know animals, plants, angels, people, and God will exist there. We know that Adam and Eve walked around in the Garden of Eden. We know that angels bow down to the throne of God. However, the Bible does not say every law of physics will be the same as it is now.

God has the power to do anything He wants, and it is so fun to see Him do it in the Bible. In 2 Kings 6, some prophets were chopping down trees to build a bigger meeting space. One of them told Elisha that the head of his borrowed ax had sunk to the bottom of a river. Elisha did what God told him to do. He cut a stick and threw it in the water where the heavy ax head sunk. It then floated to the surface. God has the power to defy gravity. So, perhaps we can still dream about flying one day in heaven.

Now, what about weather? If there is no more pain, suffering, or fear in heaven, I think we can rule out tornadoes, hurricanes, blizzards, and dangerous thunderstorms. However, we cannot rule out thunder and lightning based on this description of the throne of God.

> From the throne came flashes of lightning and the rumble of thunder. And in front of the throne were seven torches with burning flames. This is the sevenfold Spirit of God. (Revelation 4:5)

God created the water cycle where rain falls and evaporates; however, in the Garden of Eden, there was no rain. Instead, Genesis 2:5-6 says streams came up and watered the ground. Will there be rain in heaven? That might be left for us to wonder.

God also created seasons. The Bible does not specifically say they would cease to exist. Our only comparison to this new earth is our current flawed earth. We will have to see what God has planned. When I imagine the perfect weather, it would be a combination of not-too-hot and not-too-cold. The temperature would feel just right. My dear friend would disagree and say the perfect weather is cold enough for snow so she can ski in the mountains, but not too cold to be uncomfortable. The Bible does not tell us the specifics, but I imagine God will delight us all.

As for atomic power, our amazing God called into existence this entire universe with His words. I doubt we will need to worry about power sources. He is our source of power. Perhaps we will see technology beyond our imagination! Perhaps we will not need electricity at all. If the possibility of no electricity in heaven worries my friends who dream of heavenly video games, do not forget that, with words alone, God could command, "Let there be video games," and your gaming system would need nothing more to power it!

But, will He? My son certainly hopes so.

*by Susanna, 9*

# 18

## Does Heaven Have States and Countries?

Let's pause for a quick Sunday school lesson
before answering this question.

**1. What was the faith of God's Chosen People called?**
*Hint: The word starts with a J, but it isn't the
typical Sunday school answer of Jesus.*

**2. What do you call everyone who
wasn't one of the Chosen People?**
*Hint: It starts with the same sound as Jesus, but it's spelled with a G.*

<u>Answer 1</u>: If you guessed Judaism, you are correct!

God promised Abraham he would be the father of a great nation. It meant his children, grandchildren, and so on, would grow and grow in numbers. These people made up the Nation of Israel. They were God's chosen people, and they followed the religion of Judaism. Through the line, or descendants of Abraham, would come Jesus.

<u>Answer 2</u>: If you guessed Gentile, you are correct!

If you are not born Jewish, meaning you have a mother who is Jewish, then you are a Gentile. Gentiles in the Old Testament Bible times made up all the other nations. They believed in false gods, though some turned to the one true God. For example, Rahab, a Gentile from the book of Joshua, believed in God and joined the Jewish people after God saved her from the crumbling walls of Jericho. She became the mother of Boaz, who married Ruth. Ruth was the great-grandmother of King David. Jesus came through the family of David. So, you see, Jesus came from both Jews and Gentiles!

The Jews and the Gentiles were two separate groups of people. They did not typically like each other. In fact, if you were Jewish, you thought Gentiles were unclean. You would not even let them into your house, and you would not eat their food. If you were a Gentile, you might even go out of your way to avoid the Jewish people.

Jesus flipped everything upside down, inside out, and every which way by coming to save us *all*.

Still, the disciples continued seeing people as either Jew or Gentile, even after they became a Christ follower. So, in Acts 10, God put Peter into a trance, and He gave Peter a vision involving food and eating what was once considered unclean or forbidden. God told him that there was to be no more judging people to be clean and unclean based on their nation. There was no longer a need to be separate from each other. Jesus came for everyone, and Peter needed to eat with Gentiles and recognize them as brothers and sisters in Christ. He needed to share the good news of God's grace with everyone.

Can you imagine when people heard this news for the first time? I imagine there was some grumbling and arguing, especially when they realized God was instructing them to love all their neighbors. Back then, if you were a woman, a child, poor, sick, an outcast, or were different in any way, people thought you were less important. Those were the people Jesus singled out to show love, kindness, and grace. Jesus loved the children and made sure they were allowed to approach Him. He valued women and stood up for them. He was not afraid to touch those with diseases or to spend time with those who had a disability. Jesus has compassion for us all and instructs us to love even our enemies.

It took a bit of time for members of the early church to get used to this idea that God wanted them to be one family. There were still Jewish people who did not follow Jesus. There were still Gentiles who did not follow Jesus. But now there was a third group of people: Christ followers. God broke down barriers among the Christ followers. A barrier is like a wall keeping us in or out. There were both literal walls and figurative ones dividing people.

Today, we still have "walls" dividing us. People sometimes hate others for their differences. They still do not want groups of people living near them or eating with them. Our world is made up of many nations (countries), and many do not get along. There are barriers dividing countries and people. That is not God's plan for our forever life with Him. He wants us to be united and at peace as citizens of His kingdom. His invitation has been extended to everyone.

God reigns above the nations; God sits on his holy throne. (Psalm 47:8)

Can you imagine life in God's kingdom? There will be no more war, hatred, unfairness, homelessness, and strangers. One nation will exist under His just and perfect rule.

> For Christ himself has brought peace to us. He united Jews and Gentiles into one people when, in his own body on the cross, he broke down the wall of hostility that separated us. He did this by ending the system of law with its commandments and regulations. He made peace between Jews and Gentiles by creating in himself one new people from the two groups. (Ephesians 2:14-15)

This chapter goes on to describe how none of us will be foreigners or strangers.

> Together, we are his house, built on the foundation of the apostles and the prophets. And the cornerstone is Christ Jesus himself. We are carefully joined together in him, becoming a holy temple for the Lord. Through him you Gentiles are also being made part of this dwelling where God lives by his Spirit. (Ephesians2:20-21)

Have you ever felt left out or lonely? Have you ever felt like a stranger, or misunderstood? Has someone ever disliked you because of the way you look, or because of where you live? It is such an amazing treasure to know that one day we will live as a unified family where everyone belongs, nobody fights, and everyone has the best seat at the table! Together, we are God's family, or as the verse says, *"His house."* Of course, God does not mean we will be a house, but we will be part of what God is building, and Jesus is the Cornerstone.

## Wait! What is a cornerstone?

According to the Oxford Dictionary, a cornerstone is an important quality on which a particular thing depends. It also means a stone that forms the base of the corner of a building where two walls join.

We all depend on Jesus. He unites the Jews and the Gentiles like they are two walls He is joining at the corner. Christianity is built on the foundation Jesus laid, uniting us as one house, one Nation, and one Church. He is our Cornerstone.

But we are citizens of heaven, where the Lord Jesus Christ lives. And we are eagerly waiting for him to return as our Savior. He will take our weak mortal bodies and change them into glorious bodies like his own, using the same power with which he will bring everything under his control. (Philippians 3:20-21)

Have you ever felt like you did not belong? Have you felt left out? If not, have you noticed someone else being left out or someone who maybe felt like he or she did not belong? What can you do in either situation, whether it is you who is lonely, or you've noticed someone else who is lonely?

...............................................................................

...............................................................................

...............................................................................

...............................................................................

...............................................................................

...............................................................................

...............................................................................

...............................................................................

...............................................................................

...............................................................................

# 19

## Can God Talk Out Loud to You in Heaven?

The Bible describes God's voice as loud, like a trumpet in Revelation 1:10. That is an interesting description. Have you heard the music of a trumpet? Even though a trumpet is loud, its tones are beautiful and can stir emotions in us.

Imagine how you would feel if you heard a
trumpet play in the following settings?

When a king and queen
make a grand entrance ...

When an army charges into battle...

When the military song, "Taps," plays at the
end of the day or at a military funeral...

If I heard a trumpet announce royalty, I might feel a bit of excitement and awe. If a trumpet was announcing an army charge, I might feel energized or afraid, depending on which side I was on! Taps (Look up this tune if you don't know what this song is) might make me feel a bit sad, or maybe just thoughtful. I imagine when God speaks, I will feel many emotions all at once, including awe at His greatness. How about you?

Royal people may be introduced with a trumpet call, but our King of Kings needs no introduction.

> "I am the Alpha and Omega—the beginning and the end," says the Lord God. "I am the one who is, who always was, and who is still to come—the Almighty One." (Revelation 1:8)

Whatever God says is important, and these words pack a lot of meaning. What does it mean when God says He is the Alpha and Omega—beginning and end?

The symbols represent beginning and end because God is the beginning of time and end of time. He always existed outside of time. He will always exist forever.

Whew! That is a confusing idea! What is important is that God will talk to us in heaven, and He talks with us now in many ways. He communicates through the Holy Spirit. He also sent His son, Jesus, to share the Word with us. God communicates with us through the Bible and through prayer.

What are you most excited to hear God say out loud to you in heaven? I know I look forward to the words, *"Well done my good and faithful servant."*

 Check out Revelation 1:17–19 to find out what else God said to John when he got a glimpse of heaven and what job God gave the youngest of Jesus's disciples.

God, You are the beginning and the end! Your words have power. You spoke the world into creation. Forgive me when I don't listen enough to You. Please help me to understand Your words when I read my Bible. Please help me to choose my words wisely when I speak to others. Thank you for helping me learn new things. Amen

# 20

## What Does God Look Like?

This is such a fun question! First, I want to make sure we all understand that God the Father, Jesus the Son, and the Holy Spirit are equally one God and equally important. Together, they are God in three forms doing different jobs.

Through the Holy Spirit, Jesus was born to Mary as both God and a man. That is a difficult truth to wrap our heads around! Jesus brought us the Word of God, written by men who were directed and inspired by the Holy Spirit. Jesus rose from the dead and returned to sit at the right hand of the Father. According to Psalm 47:8, the Father sits on His holy throne, and Jesus sits at His right hand. Jesus sent the Holy Spirit to be with all of us and dwell (live) in us.

One of my Sunday school friends asked me if the three would be one form in heaven. It is a fascinating idea, but no. All three forms of God existed from the beginning of time, and all three will exist forever. John 1:1 said Jesus and God were there in the beginning, and while God was creating the universe, Genesis 1:2 says, "and the Spirit of God was hovering over the waters."

Also, when John saw the throne of God, he saw Jesus separate from God and he recognized his Savior and friend. When Jesus was in our world, He had a familiar and beloved human face that the disciples knew well. John loved Jesus so much, he even claimed favorite student status in his Gospel by referring to himself as *"the beloved disciple!"* John would have memorized the face of Jesus.

When John saw Jesus in His heavenly form, John knew Jesus. The Bible says in Revelation 1:17 that John fell at his feet as if dead! Let's find out what he saw. There are some confusing descriptions, so don't worry about it if you don't quite understand. These descriptions might be literal, but they also might be symbolic. I will explain that in a bit.

> And standing in the middle of the lampstands was someone like the Son of Man. He was wearing a long robe with a gold sash across his chest. His head and his hair were white like wool, as white as snow. And his eyes were like flames of fire. His feet were like polished bronze refined in a furnace, and his voice thundered like mighty ocean waves. He held seven stars in his right hand, and a sharp two-edged sword came from his mouth. And his face was like the sun in all its brilliance. When I saw him, I fell at his feet as if I were dead. But he laid his right hand on me and said, "Don't be afraid! I am the First and the Last. I am the living one. I died, but look—I am alive forever and ever! And I hold the keys of death and the grave. (Revelation 1:13–18)

In verse 19, Jesus told John to write down what he saw so we all could understand too. Have you ever returned from vacation and tried to share the experiences with others who were not there? It is not quite as exciting to hear it second-hand. They missed out on being there. Still, when I hear someone describing a cool place, I find myself wanting to go there as well. When I read this passage, I want so much to be there and to see this for myself!

I certainly am glad Jesus wanted John to tell us what we might expect one day so we too can look forward to seeing Jesus in His heavenly form. What an amazing thing Jesus revealed to John and to us! Does this make you so excited to see what John saw with your own eyes?

His word pictures are great, but they do require some close reading, because they can mean more than one thing. We can read these descriptions as literal (John really did see these things as he describes), but God also wants us to understand even more meaning from them through their symbolism. Symbolism is the use of pictures, words, or symbols to help us understand an idea.

For example, John described Jesus as having a two-edged sword coming from his mouth. John literally saw this, but God wants us to recognize more meanings too. Here are two ways we could read it.

Meaning: Jesus is the Word, and the sword often represents the message He brought.

Meaning: Jesus is the Great Judge of humankind, and He will battle evil and win.

 You can read Hebrews 4:12–13 to learn more about the double–edged sword. Jesus was not the conqueror of nations that the Jewish people wanted when they imagined their Savior and King. Instead, He conquered sin.

John also described Jesus as having *eyes like flames of fire.*

This was what he literally saw, but there are symbolic meanings too relating to Jesus being a righteous (right and fair) judge of the world who will send people to a very real hell.

**Will Jesus look like this all the time in heaven?**

The Bible does not say, so we will have to wait until we get there. When I picture Jesus, He looks warmer and fuzzier, like the *"Come here and give me a big hug"* Jesus, rather than the *"I can cut you down with this sword"* Jesus. Either way, the Bible reminds us in Revelation 19:16, that written on His robe at his thigh, Jesus will have the name "King of Kings and Lord of Lords." This may be the biggest name tag we have ever seen!

No matter what He looks like, there will be no mistaking Jesus, our Lord and King. We must never forget; our warm and fuzzy savior also is a mighty warrior and Lord of All. He is our friend who loves us, but He also is fierce and powerful. I certainly am glad I am on His side!

There are so many more cool details in these verses! For example, it says Jesus was standing by lampstands. Any time you see the description of lampstands in Revelation, it also may be talking about churches. Jesus represents the Church, or all believers.

Did you also notice how Jesus said, *"Don't be afraid, I am the first and the last?"* Do you recall our lesson right before this one on Alpha and Omega? God is the first and the last. It is cool that Jesus reminds us here that He is God, and God is the beginning and end. He existed before we did, and He will always exist.

We have seen through John's eyes what Jesus looks like, but he also gives us a glimpse of God's throne. According to Revelation 4:3, John described God as "brilliant as gemstones" with the glow of an emerald circling God's throne like a rainbow. From the throne he described seeing flashes of lightning and the rumbling of thunder. That sounds like quite the scene!

God told Moses in Exodus 33:20 that nobody could look at His face and live. Moses entered God's presence, but God had to protect him from getting a good look. Even then, Moses glowed after his encounter with God. This is important, because when we get to heaven, things will be different. Moses could not look at God's face, but we will get to be in God's presence and Revelation 22:4 says we will see His face, and His name will be on our foreheads. We will be able to approach His throne with confidence because of what Jesus did for us by dying on a cross and rising from the dead three days later!

**How do we know we can trust John's vision, though?**

Did you know John is not the only witness to this amazing sight? Long before John was born, a guy named Ezekiel also had a vision of heaven, and he too saw God's throne with a figure like that of a man on it. Ezekiel also was so awed; he fell face down on the ground in worship and reverence.

> From what appeared to be his waist up, he looked like gleaming amber, flickering like a fire. And from his waist down, he looked like a burning flame, shining with splendor. All around him was a glowing halo, like a rainbow shining in the clouds on a rainy day. This is what the glory of the Lord looked like to me. When I saw it, I fell face down on the ground, and I heard someone's voice speaking to me. (Ezekiel 1:27–28)

It is interesting to note that both men described God on His throne with colors. I like that.

Have you seen the movie, *"The Wizard of Oz?"* It starts out in black and white. Then, the main character, Dorothy, reaches this magical world of Oz and everything appears in color. She searches for the Emerald City, which is represented by the color emerald green. That is a made-up story, though imagine if what we see now is like looking at a world in black and white, and one day our eyes will be opened to a brilliant burst of color as we reach the throne of God! We haven't even begun to experience the beauty that is to come!

Meanwhile, God has given us plenty of colors to enjoy. My daughter has always enjoyed asking people what their favorite color is. It is hard to have just one favorite color, because so many are pretty. When she doesn't feel like choosing one, she will say she likes the rainbow and choose them all.

What is your favorite color?

Speaking of color, I bet I can stump you with some fun trivia questions below!

---

Trivia Time! True or false?

1. If you mix every paint color of the rainbow together, you get white paint.

2. If you mix red, green, and blue light, you get white light.

3. Roy G. Biv invented color.

*(Answers are at the bottom of the next page.)*

---

How does the story of Noah relate to the topic of heaven? Why do you think God chose colors to represent his promise/covenant in Genesis 9:12–17?

........................................................................

........................................................................

........................................................................

........................................................................

........................................................................

........................................................................

........................................................................

........................................................................

........................................................................

........................................................................

........................................................................

........................................................................

........................................................................

........................................................................

Answers: **1**. False. You will get gray. No amount of color mixing makes white paint. It is different when light mixes to make white light. **2**. True. Red, green, and blue light will make white light. **3**. False: This is just a fun way to remember the colors God created in a rainbow: **R**ed, **O**range, **Y**ellow, **G**reen, **B**lue, **I**ndigo, and **V**iolet.

# 21

## If God Writes Our Name on His Hand, Can He Erase It? Can We Decide to be Erased?

See, I have written your name on the palms of my hands. (Isaiah 49:16)

When you become a believer in Jesus Christ, your name is written on the palms of His hands. It's a very important symbol, but what does it mean?

> Quiz time! Why do you think the verse mentions the palms of Jesus's hands here? Choose the best answer:
>
> A. Jesus wants us to think about Him every time we wash our hands.
> B. Jesus was all out of stone tablets, so He wrote on His hand instead.
> C. His Book of Life was already full.
> D. Our crucified Jesus had nails pierce the palms of His hands when He willingly went to the cross *for us* to save us from our sins.

If you guessed "D" you are correct! After Jesus rose from the dead, John 20:27 says the disciple Thomas would not believe Jesus was alive until he saw the scars on His hands. The blood Jesus shed for us means we belong to Jesus permanently. Our names won't be erased.

While our names are on God's hands, it says in Revelation 22:4, that God's name will be written on our forehead! This might be symbolic, or we might literally have a marking on our forehead proclaiming we belong to God. Have you ever seen those sticker nametags, "Hello my name is..." and then you write in your name? I imagine that nametag smack dab on my forehead.

Hello my name is:

Child of the King of Kings.

So, can a follower of Jesus decide to no longer follow God after God's name is written on his or her forehead?

When you become a follower of Jesus, you want to be different. You become a new creation in Him. You receive the Holy Spirit, and you belong to God forever. If you mess up, you are still a child of God. There is a big difference between making a sinful mistake and continuing the same sin without being sorry about it.

> Anyone who continues to live in Him will not sin. But anyone who keeps on sinning does not know Him or understand who He is. (1 John 3:6)

When you decide to follow Jesus, the evidence is a changed life. It does not mean you won't sin. Sometimes, people even go through times when they are not close with the Lord. But, once you turn from your sin, the Holy Spirit will guide you and help you. God will never stop pursuing you. No matter how many mistakes you make, when you repent (ask God to forgive you), He gives you grace. But don't take my word for it. Read it for yourself!

Check out John 10:27–30. Can anyone snatch us from God? Also, read Ephesians 3:14–21. I hope the apostle Paul's beautiful words encourage you to grow in your faith. This would be a great section to highlight in your Bible!

# 22

## God Says He Loves Everybody, So Does God Love Satan? Could God and Satan Be Friends in the End?

Let me challenge you with another question before we answer this one.

**Question: Who is the opposite of God?**

If you guessed Satan, it would make sense. Satan is all things evil. God is all things good. However, Satan is *not* the correct answer. Satan was created by God. He is an angel. God created angels, and they can *never* be equal to God. Satan, known as Lucifer, was a powerful angel, and Satan wanted to be the ruler of all. He is described symbolically in the book of Ezekiel.

> ... I ordained and anointed you as the mighty angelic guardian. You had access to the holy mountain of God and walked among the stones of fire. You were blameless in all you did from the day you were created until the day evil was found in you. (Ezekiel 28:14–15)

It goes on to say pride and greed made Satan violent and led him to sin. He was kicked out and banished from the "Mountain of God." Isaiah 14 also symbolically describes Satan. It says he wanted to make himself like God and even more important, or higher, than God.

God is the Alpha and Omega. He already knows what will happen. He has allowed Satan to cause destruction in our world for now, but one day soon, God will destroy Satan and judge all those who stood with Satan. They will not be friends.

Do not miss this!

Satan and God are on opposite sides, but they are not opposites. There is no equal to God. There are no other gods. He is above all. God can't have an opposite.

People must choose on which side they want to belong. You are either for God and *good* or you are for Satan and *evil*. That sounds harsh, but there is no in-between. The good news is we know which side will be victorious. Good wins. Evil loses.

Satan has fooled a lot of people into joining his side. Thankfully, God loves us so much that He has been patiently giving people time to switch sides and choose Jesus. God does not force people to choose to love Him, but He is very clear about our need for a Savior.

Jesus replied, "I tell you the truth, unless you are born again, you cannot see the Kingdom of God." (John 3:3)

God sent his Son into the world not to judge the world, but to save the world through him. There is no judgement against anyone who believes in him. But anyone who does not believe in him has already been judged for not believing in God's one and only Son. And the judgment is based on this fact: God's light came into the world, but people loved the darkness more than the light, for their actions were evil. All who do evil hate the light and refuse to go near it for fear their sins will be exposed. But those who do what is right come to the light so others can see that they are doing what God wants. (John 3:17-21)

After Jesus comes back, there will be a great battle against Satan. Michael the Archangel will be leading the battle. Michael is described as one who stands guard over Israel. Satan, once a mighty cherub, is described in this next verse as a dragon thrown down to earth. Satan also is described as a serpent slithering on the ground in the Garden of Eden. His followers are angels who chose evil and are referred to as demons.

Then there was war in heaven. Michael and his angels fought against the dragon and his angels. And the dragon lost the battle, and he and his angels were forced out of heaven. This great dragon—the ancient serpent called the devil, or Satan, the one deceiving the whole world—was thrown down to the earth with all his angels. (Revelation 12:7-9)

Satan chose evil, and the Bible says he will one day be defeated and thrown into a lake of fire. The demons will be judged and punished. Those who reject Jesus will face judgement and hell. Only those who choose Jesus, and His gift of salvation, will be counted as friends.

Check out Daniel 12:1–4. What will happen to God's people according to this passage? How does it make you feel to know that God has a rescue plan in place for us?

# 23

## Do We Have Needs Like Hunger and Thirst? If Not, Will We Still Eat?

One sad thing about our world is that there are many people who are hungry or starving. There are places where people also do not have access to clean drinking water. They are thirsty. This will not be so in heaven.

> They will never again be hungry or thirsty; they will never be scorched by the heat of the sun. (Revelation 7:16)

This passage does not answer whether we will *need* food and water like our human bodies; however, it says we will not go without as so many do on this broken earth.

So, will there be food and drinks at all in heaven?

In Luke 24:43 the resurrected Jesus asked the disciples for food. That tells us two things:

1. He could eat.

2. He possibly felt hungry.

To clarify, by hungry, I mean the kind like, "A burger and fries sounds really good right now," and not the kind that means starving. There is satisfaction in eating a good meal until you feel full. Don't you think? If we never felt a little hungry, we would never want to eat anything.

In the Garden of Eden, you might recall that God provided

Adam and Eve with food, including fruit trees. Eating was part of their daily lives. In Revelation 19:7–10 it says we will be invited to a great wedding feast prepared for us in heaven. We will sit at God's table. I cannot imagine a feast without food and drinks.

If you were sitting at the banquet table right now, what would your drink order be?

a. Hot chocolate
b. Apple juice
c. Pop (I'm from Ohio. I can't in good conscience call it soda.)
d. Fruit punch
e. A sports drink
f. Flavored water
g. Other

My choice might depend on what the main course is, though right now I think I would go for the hot chocolate. It would be impossible for us to begin to imagine the feast and delights prepared for us at God's table! I imagine a lot of laughter, conversation, and a feeling of honor to be given a seat at such a magnificent event. This is not in the Bible, of course, but I am imagining a never-ending supply of tasty desserts. That would be "heavenly!" What do you imagine or wonder?

Check out Matthew 22:1–24. Jesus used a parable (lesson) about a wedding feast to help us understand His invitation into the Kingdom of Heaven.

Just for fun...

1.  If you could eat just one food for the rest of forever, what would it be?

2.  If God asked you what you wanted for dinner, what would you request?

3.  If you had a choice to sit by anyone in all of history, which two people would you want on either side of you at the banquet table?

# 24

## Will You Be Able to See, Visit, or Communicate with People Back on Earth?

It is so hard to say "goodbye for now" to people we love. I often imagine that my loved ones in heaven can see highlights of what is going on down here. The Bible does not tell us for sure. At least among the angels there is awareness of what we are up to here on earth.

> ...there is joy in the presence of God's angels when even one sinner repents. (Luke 15:10)

Whether or not people in heaven know what is happening in our lives, there will be plenty of time in eternity for us to share memories when we all are together one day. The cool thing about heaven is that we will not feel sad, so our loved ones are not up there feeling like they are missing out on life here. It is harder for us here because we miss those who have gone before us.

Some people believe they are visited by loved ones who have died. Some even believe there are souls haunting places and people. This is not in the Bible. Once people die, they do not have the choice to hang out where they want, or to avoid God's judgment. You are not lost somewhere in between. You also will not go from heaven back to earth. Jesus reassures us of this.

> No one has ever gone to heaven and returned. But the
> Son of Man has come down from heaven. (John 3:13)

In the Bible, God communicated with people through prophets, dreams, angels, and even with His voice. Then, He spoke to us through Jesus and His Word.

> Long ago God spoke many times and in many ways
> to us our ancestors through the prophets. And now
> in these final days, he has spoken to us through his
> Son. (Hebrews 1:1–2)

God does _not_ need our help communicating His will. He does _not_ need the help of our loved ones to convince us to follow Him. He told us what is going to happen when He returns for us, so we do _not_ need the help of anyone to tell us the future.

**What about those people who claim to be able to speak to the dead?**

There are examples in the Bible of people attempting to speak to the dead, but this is through evil, and not God. God warns us against such actions. We *never* want to give Satan and his demons power over us.

> ... And do not let your people practice fortune-telling,
> or use sorcery, or interpret omens, or engage in
> witchcraft, or cast spells, or function as mediums
> or psychics, or call forth the spirits of the dead.
> (Deuteronomy 18:10–11)

There definitely are people that call on Satan to help them try to see the future or to speak to the dead. This happened in the Bible in 1 Samuel 28. Saul desperately wanted to know the future, so he broke his own law that banned the practice of telling fortunes or speaking to people who died. They called these spirit-seeking people mediums. Saul convinced a medium to speak to the prophet Samuel, but it is more likely he spoke to Satan in disguise. Instead of comforting him, the message left him more distressed than satisfied.

When we call on Satan, we give him access to our lives, and we open ourselves up to his lies. In 2 Corinthians 11:14, the Bible tells us Satan "disguises himself as an angel of light." He can seem fun, safe, and good.

Satan is sneaky and likes when we feel sad, lonely, or when we are looking for comfort. He knows we have a choice. We can ask God to be our comforter, provider, truth, and healer, or we could ask Satan to give us what might feel good in the moment, but it will not bring us peace, or strength, or even hope.

It is difficult when we miss people we love. I know I dream of being able to talk to them again. However, it is important to trust God when He reassures us that our day of reunion is coming. In the meantime, He calls us to obedience. That means trusting Him and not letting Satan tempt you with lies. It means not trusting people to read your fortune. Don't play with cards claiming to predict your future. Don't try to get spirits to talk to you. These things are all from Satan.

If you find yourself wishing to be able to talk to the person you love, try writing in a journal. It helps to be able to put thoughts into writing, and it is a good way to work through our sadness. As a kid, I used to write letters to loved ones that died. Even though I knew they were not reading them, it made me feel like I was still able to talk to them. It helped me feel less sad over time. At some point, I no longer needed to write those letters.

When you are sad, you can also talk to God. I tell Him the things I wish I could say to that person who is no longer here with me. He is always willing to listen, and He understands my sadness. I ask Him to help me with my sadness, or grief. He really does! When we cry out to God, He not only listens, but He answers us. He provides for all our needs, and that includes our need for comfort. God is the Great Comforter! Goodbyes, even when temporary, are hard. Praise God, He never leaves us, no matter what! We can always count on Him to be with us.

Do you miss someone who has died? What has helped you in your sadness? Put a checkmark next to the things that help you feel better, and if you are not sure, maybe you can try one or two out to see if they help you. If you have not experienced the death of a loved one yet, I am so glad. Perhaps you can share these ideas with someone who has.

◊ Write in a journal.

◊ Write a letter, even though you can't actually send it.

◊ Talk to God about your sadness.

◊ Talk to someone who knew the person you miss and share special memories.

◊ Draw a picture of that person in heaven surrounded by what brought them joy here in this life.

◊ Write a poem about how you feel.

◊ Talk to a trusted adult about your feelings.

◊ Do something nice for others in memory of that person.

◊ Remind yourself it is OK if you need to cry. Even Jesus wept when His good friend died. (John 11:35). Go find someone you trust and let them know you are sad and if you need a hug while you cry.

Check out 1 Corinthians 15:35–58 and be encouraged that death is not the end! Who are you looking forward to seeing again one day soon?

....................................................................

....................................................................

....................................................................

....................................................................

....................................................................

....................................................................

....................................................................

....................................................................

....................................................................

....................................................................

....................................................................

....................................................................

....................................................................

....................................................................

....................................................................

....................................................................

....................................................................

....................................................................

# 25

## If We Are No Longer Sinners in Heaven, Is It Physically Impossible for Us to Do Something Wrong?

For example, if we try to hit someone, would our hand just freeze? If we tried to say a bad word, would our mouth not work?

This question makes me giggle just a bit. I am picturing a brother and sister racing around attempting to swat at each other just to see their hands freeze in the air.

The Bible is clear that we must be made clean and right (righteous) through the blood of Jesus, and we will no longer sin. That temptation to sin (fueled by our sinful nature and by Satan) will no longer be a part of us. I think it is safe to assume you would not *want* to hit someone. Your heart will be so full of joy, love, and praise for our God, you will not have bad thoughts. You will not be angry, scared, annoyed, in pain, or afraid.

Instead, your focus will be on the awesomeness of the life God has created for you in His kingdom.

Can you imagine a place where everyone is loving and kind? Your feelings are never hurt in heaven. You are never left out, never teased, and never wounded. You are safe. You are cherished. You are filled with peace. Best of all, you will have no end to joy, fun, and laughter. There will be no sadness or death.

*He will wipe every tear from their eyes, and there will be no more death or sorrow or crying or pain. All these things are gone forever.* (Revelation 21:4)

## Sorry, not sorry!

Do you have siblings or close friends with whom you tend to squabble?

- What are some of the disagreements/fights you have most often?
- How does that person hurt you, and how do you hurt them?
- What are some ways you can change this pattern to instead reflect Christ in both your actions and responses?

1. He/She bothers me most when…

_____

_____

2. I usually respond by… _____

_____

_____

3. After talking to God about it, I think maybe I should change by …

_____

_____

4. What will your relationship look like in heaven without sin?

_____

_____

God, thank you that You designed us to enjoy humor and laughter. We look forward to the day when we can laugh and enjoy time spent in Your joy and peace. Meanwhile, please help us when we are tempted to sin. Sometimes it is difficult to get along with others—especially since we all are sinners. Please help us grow in our self-control and kindness, even when it is so hard sometimes. Amen!

# 26

## Is It Possible to Visit Heaven and Come Back?

"Heaven tourism" is a term people have used to describe those who claim to have died and visited heaven, but then were revived, or brought back to life here on earth. There are people out there writing books, speaking to groups, and creating movies about their near-death experiences. Some say they were given a choice to come back or stay.

However, Jesus clearly states in John 3:13 that you cannot go to heaven and come back. I also think it is safe to say that once you see heaven, you will not want to come back!

So, why is it that some people in the Bible, like John and Ezekiel, got "tours" of heaven? Was this different?

These two men, while in the Spirit, were given revelations by God. They did not claim to die and come back to life. They revealed only what God wanted them to reveal. Their visions and prophecies of heaven were not focused on themselves.

Because God has already revealed heaven to us, we do not need any more information. We must be on our guard against any new revelations people claim to have. God warns us about trying to add to His complete Word.

And I solemnly declare to everyone who hears the words of prophecy written in this book: If anyone

adds anything to what is written here, God will add
to that person the plagues described in this book.
(Revelation 22:18)

I sure do miss people very much, and I wish I could talk to them or visit with them until it is my turn to join them in heaven. Let's imagine, though, that we were able to talk to someone in heaven for just a moment. What would we say? What could we possibly tell that person that God has not already told them? What could we ask that God has not already told us, or promises to tell us one day soon?

Heaven can certainly feel a long way away. Have you ever been on a vacation, or were visiting a cousin or a good friend, and it felt like there was not enough time for all the fun you were having? All good adventures and play dates must come to an end.

But, what if they did not have to end? What if you could hang out as long as you wanted—even as long as forever? I am looking forward to the time we will spend in our forever home visiting with each other and having adventures. We will have as much time as we want to reconnect, share stories, and make new memories. Until then, we won't be able to see or talk to our loved ones who went home to Jesus before us.

When you long to be able to communicate with someone who has died, call out to God instead. Ask the Holy Spirit for comfort and peace. Tell God the message you wish you could share. He is listening. He cares. He loves the ones you miss, and He understands your pain.

God hates death. The good news is, God has defeated death and has rescued us!

Check out Psalm 4 and underline the verses that bring you the most comfort. I underlined that God hears me when I call on Him. I also especially like verse 8. What do you think about it?

..............................................................

..............................................................

..............................................................

..............................................................

..............................................................

..............................................................

..............................................................

..............................................................

..............................................................

..............................................................

..............................................................

..............................................................

..............................................................

..............................................................

..............................................................

..............................................................

..............................................................

..............................................................

# 27

## Do You Sleep in Heaven?
## Do You Dream?

I think this question is going to fall under the category of "mystery." The Bible, as far as I am aware, does not say. If you find a verse somewhere, let me know! We know for sure we will be restored to new and perfect bodies, so we will not grow weary. I look forward to having energy without fatigue, but will we need sleep?

Our brains dream at night as we process information. Perhaps we will be able to process that information without sleep. Or, perhaps a few cat naps will still be beneficial. Sometimes dreams are bad—like nightmares. I can say for certain that nightmares are not part of God's perfect plan in heaven. I can also say that if you have ever spent hours lying awake trying to sleep, and have felt frustrated that you could not, that won't be an issue either!

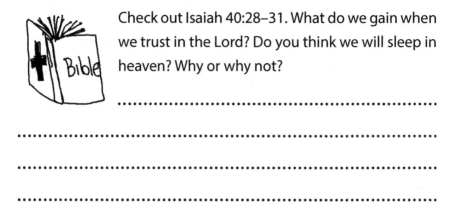

Check out Isaiah 40:28–31. What do we gain when we trust in the Lord? Do you think we will sleep in heaven? Why or why not?

...........................................................

...........................................................

...........................................................

...........................................................

# 28

## Do You Have Emotions in Heaven?

God created you to be emotional. You have emotions like joy, happiness, and excitement. You also experience emotions like sorrow, fear, anger, and jealousy.

Based on what you have learned so far in this study of heaven, which emotions do you think will be absent from heaven?

If you guessed the painful and uncomfortable emotions, I would agree with you. Emotions in themselves are not bad, but what we do with them can be sinful. They can lead to things like jealousy and rage, or sadness and fear. Thankfully, we will no longer feel that way in heaven.

> He will wipe away every tear from their eyes. There will be no more death or mourning or crying or pain, for the old has passed away. (Revelation 21:4)

God created us to be emotional. Just because we will be transformed in heaven with new bodies, it does not mean we will stop being who we are. You are unique. God made you with a personality, gifts, and abilities. Although God will free us from sin, God will not erase who we are. He wants us to be delighted. He wants us to feel awe, wonder, and joy. Most of all, He wants us to feel His love. He could have created robots. He could have forced everyone to obey Him, but He did not. God chose us, and He allowed us to choose Him. What joy we will have when we stand before His throne worshipping with countless believers! Glory to God in the highest! He is worthy of our praise!

Check out Psalm 139. How well does the God who created you *know you* and your emotions?

.........................................................................

.........................................................................

.........................................................................

.........................................................................

.........................................................................

.........................................................................

.........................................................................

.........................................................................

.........................................................................

.........................................................................

.........................................................................

.........................................................................

.........................................................................

.........................................................................

.........................................................................

.........................................................................

.........................................................................

# 29

## Will You Still Be the Same Age as When You Die? Can You Grow up in Heaven? Will Everyone Be Old?

In 1 Corinthians 15, we learn all about our resurrected bodies. I encourage you to read the whole chapter. In a nutshell, we have been given earthly bodies, but when Jesus comes back, we will have heavenly (resurrected) bodies.

> Our bodies are buried in brokenness, but they will be raised in glory. They are buried in weakness, but they will be raised in strength. (1 Corinthians 15:43)

Our broken earthly bodies die. They cannot live forever. We will get our new bodies when Jesus returns. Some of us will be with Jesus already at the time He comes back. Others may still be living here in our broken world.

> But let me reveal to you a wonderful secret. We will not all die, but we will all be transformed! It will happen in a moment, in the blink of an eye, when the last trumpet is blown. For when the trumpet sounds, those who have died will be raised to live forever. And we who are living will also be transformed. For our dying bodies must be transformed into bodies that

will never die; our mortal bodies must be transformed into immortal bodies.

Then, when our dying bodies have been transformed into bodies that will never die, this Scripture will be fulfilled:

"Death is swallowed up in victory.
O death, where is your victory?
O death, where is your sting?" (1 Corinthians 15:51–55)

**We get a new body, but how old do you think we will all appear in heaven?**

Let me ask you another question. How old do you feel right now? If you did not have a mirror or a calendar, do you think you would feel your age? What does 7 feel like? How about 10 or 12? When you wake up on your birthday do you feel older?

My grandmother, who went home to be with Jesus at age 92, said she never felt her age. In her mind, she was still a young woman. When she gets her new resurrected body upon the return of Jesus, she will not feel 92. She will have the same wisdom and knowledge she gained in those years, but gone will be the achy body, the wrinkles, and the need for hearing aids.

While the Bible does not say how old we all will look in our new bodies, it will not matter. We will never stop gaining new knowledge or making new memories. Our brains will keep operating. Remember, God did not create us to be mindless robots. We will not stop being who we are simply because we are in heaven. We will be our best selves without sin.

What about babies and young children?

I imagine those babies will continue to grow in wisdom, memories, and knowledge along with the rest of us. Jesus came to our world as a baby, but He did not cease being God.

Jesus grew in wisdom and in stature and in favor with God and all the people. (Luke 2:52)

Eternity is a long time. When we reach adulthood here, we stop growing, and our bodies start to slowly wear out. This will not happen with our new bodies. So, will we all be old? I think in our current measurement of years, yes. In our minds, I think we will feel as we feel now: simply ourselves, but smarter, because our brains will be in top condition! I am glad of this since I certainly am forgetful. I look forward to learning everyone's names in heaven and not forgetting them! Are you good at remembering names? That is a gift!

God, we thank You and praise You that You are making all things new, including our bodies! Please help us to take good care of our earthly bodies, and no matter our age, please help us to continue to grow in wisdom, knowledge, and love for You. Amen!

# 30

## In Heaven, Are You Like a Ghost, or Do You Have a Body?

Yes. You will have an actual body in heaven. If you are asking if our body will be transparent, like what we imagine for a ghost, that is an interesting thought. Let's read about some things that took place after Jesus died and came back to life.

> That Sunday evening the disciples were meeting behind locked doors because they were afraid of the Jewish leaders. Suddenly, Jesus was standing there among them! "Peace be with you," he said. (John 20:19)

Somehow Jesus appeared in the room. It does not say He walked through the walls, but it also does not say He opened the locked door and entered. The disciple, Thomas, doubted what his friends told him because he had not been there. He would believe, he said, if he could touch the hands where Jesus had been nailed to a cross and see where His side had been pierced. A week later, Jesus again came into the room despite the locked door. However, this time Jesus told Thomas he could touch Him.

The disciples, like you, wondered if Jesus was a ghost. Jesus made sure they understood He was real, solid, and alive.

> "Why are you frightened?" he asked. "Why are your hearts filled with doubt? Look at my hands. Look at

my feet. You can see that it's really me. Touch me and make sure that I am not a ghost, because ghosts don't have bodies, as you see that I do." As he spoke, he showed them his hands and his feet.

Still they stood there in disbelief, filled with joy and wonder. Then he asked them, "Do you have anything here to eat?" They gave him a piece of broiled fish, and he ate it as they watched. (Luke 24:38–43)

Poor Thomas earned the nickname, "Doubting Thomas," because he wanted proof before he would believe. I can relate to Thomas. Can you? Thankfully, Jesus knew we would want proof. The disciples were first-hand witnesses to Jesus and his resurrected body. They saw Him. They spoke with Him. They watched Him *eat food*. This proof that Jesus was not a ghost was so important, because as you know, there are still people who say Jesus did not rise from the dead.

Let's recap what we now know.

1. We will have bodies that are solid and can eat.
2. We will not be ghosts.
3. We may be able to move from one place to another in unique ways. Perhaps Jesus walked through the wall. Perhaps He teleported. I am excited to find out one day.

God, thanks for giving us perfect bodies in heaven. Thanks also for providing us with proof that You are real and that You love us. Even though You do not always give us every answer we want to know, we are thankful for all that You have revealed to us through Jesus and the Bible. Amen!

# 31

## Will You Be Fat or Skinny in Heaven?

When you think of a beautiful body, what do you imagine? Unfortunately, people often have in mind specific body shapes and sizes when they decide what is or is not beautiful/handsome. Thankfully, we know the truth. God made us in His image, as the Bible tells us.

> So God created human beings in his own image. In the image of God he created them; male and female he created them. (Genesis 1:27)

If we are made in God's image, we are beautifully and wonderfully made. No matter what *people* think of our outward appearance, *God* thinks we are beautiful.

God gave us our bodies and wants us to take good care of ourselves. To be healthy we need to do the following:

1. Eat a well-balanced nutritious diet.
2. Get regular doctor checkups.
3. Exercise.
4. Wear sunscreen and other sun protection.
5. Take showers. ;)

Speaking of healthy ...

* Would you rather have a bad cold/flu virus for 10 days or the stomach flu where you vomit repeatedly for 24 hours?
* Would you rather run 100 miles or swim with a bunch of jellyfish?
* Would you rather eat only vegetables for a week or lose your voice for two days?
* Would you rather take gross-flavored medicine or get a shot?

Even if we do all the right things to stay healthy, our bodies still fail us. Our bodies still age and get sick. Some people struggle with extra weight and some with not enough weight. In heaven, our bodies will be perfectly healthy. We will not judge each other based on our flawed sinful thinking. Whether we all will be the same size, or whether we will be diverse like we are now, we all will be equally beautiful in the eyes of God and each other. I love that!

Have you ever struggled with your appearance? I used to dislike my nose. Why? It is a perfectly normal nose. However, I sometimes felt like it was too long, too narrow, and too freckled. The funny thing is, if I could change my nose right now, I would not. It is my nose. It is just the way God designed it to be. Unfortunately, I spent way too much time as a tween/teen worrying about things like pimples, body shape, and bad haircuts. Sometimes, it was because other kids teased me. Sometimes, it was because I felt like I needed to look a certain way. I wish I could have trusted that God made me beautiful just the way I was. I would have saved so much time spent worrying and trying to change myself.

How about you? Do you believe you are beautiful or handsome?

I pray as you grow in love, joy, peace, patience, kindness, goodness, faithfulness, gentleness, and self–control, you recognize your beauty/handsomeness comes from within, and that you see yourself how God sees you.

 Check out 1 Samuel 16:7. Samuel was looking for the future king, and while all David's brothers were taller, bigger, and more royal looking, David was the one God chose. Why was this, according to the Bible?

In one box below, write about or draw the things you do not like about the way you were made. Do you wish your eyes were a different color, or that you were more athletic? Do you dislike your nose, or wish you were taller or shorter?

In the other box, remind yourself what God sees and believes about you. Ask God to help you see yourself as beautiful or handsome—the way He sees you.

| How I see me. | How God sees me. |
| --- | --- |
|  |  |
|  |  |
|  |  |
|  |  |

Check out 2 Corinthians 5:6–10. Why should we live by believing and not by seeing? What should be our focus and goal?

· · · · · · · · · · · · · · · · · · · · · · · · · · · · · · · · · · · · · · · · · · ·

· · · · · · · · · · · · · · · · · · · · · · · · · · · · · · · · · · · · · · · · · · · · · · · · ·

· · · · · · · · · · · · · · · · · · · · · · · · · · · · · · · · · · · · · · · · · · · · · · · · ·

· · · · · · · · · · · · · · · · · · · · · · · · · · · · · · · · · · · · · · · · · · · · · · · · ·

· · · · · · · · · · · · · · · · · · · · · · · · · · · · · · · · · · · · · · · · · · · · · · · · ·

· · · · · · · · · · · · · · · · · · · · · · · · · · · · · · · · · · · · · · · · · · · · · · · · ·

· · · · · · · · · · · · · · · · · · · · · · · · · · · · · · · · · · · · · · · · · · · · · · · · ·

· · · · · · · · · · · · · · · · · · · · · · · · · · · · · · · · · · · · · · · · · · · · · · · · ·

· · · · · · · · · · · · · · · · · · · · · · · · · · · · · · · · · · · · · · · · · · · · · · · · ·

· · · · · · · · · · · · · · · · · · · · · · · · · · · · · · · · · · · · · · · · · · · · · · · · ·

· · · · · · · · · · · · · · · · · · · · · · · · · · · · · · · · · · · · · · · · · · · · · · · · ·

· · · · · · · · · · · · · · · · · · · · · · · · · · · · · · · · · · · · · · · · · · · · · · · · ·

Thank you, God, for creating us to be beautiful. We are made in Your image, and You make no mistakes. Please help us to see ourselves as You see us, and please help us recognize what makes us beautiful—our hearts. Please help us to become more beautiful the more we grow in our faith and our love for You. In the precious name of Jesus, we pray. Amen!

# 32

## Can You Get Married or Have Babies in Heaven?

The religious leaders had this same question for Jesus. They asked what would happen if a woman's husbands kept dying and she kept remarrying. Who would be her husband at the resurrection? Jesus said this:

> For when the dead rise, they will neither marry nor be given in marriage. In this respect they will be like the angels in heaven. (Matthew 22:30)

It is so nice when we get such a clear answer to a question! There is no marriage in heaven, and because of that, people will not have more children. I will still love my husband, but we will not be married in heaven. My children will still be my children, but more importantly, they will be children of God just like me. Our focus will not be on our own family unit, but instead will be on this huge family of God to which we belong.

In Genesis 1:28 God blessed Adam and Eve and told them to be fruitful and multiply (have lots of kids). This does not mean that everyone on earth will get married, nor will everyone have children. God has a special plan for each of us! God gave them that blessing, because He wants the earth to be filled with His children, and He wants them to know and love Him.

In Matthew 28, Jesus reminds us that on this earth our purpose is to share His truth.

> Therefore, go and make disciples of all the nations, baptizing them in the name of the Father and the Son and the Holy Spirit. Teach these new disciples to obey all the commands I have given you. And be sure of this: I am with you always, even to the end of the age. (Matthew 28:19–20)

Whatever our situation was on earth, our new focus at the resurrection will be living alongside our amazing God, serving Him, worshipping Him, and delighting in all He has planned for us. I hope this is a comfort to you. Change is hard for my kids, and this idea that our family will be different in heaven is somewhat upsetting for them. But don't forget, in heaven you will not have worries and fears, so change will be exciting!

Dear Jesus, please help us to focus on You and Your love for us, rather than on our worries about what might be different in heaven. We can't even begin to grasp how much better everything will be one day when we are with You, so please help us to trust You and Your plan for our forever. Amen!

# 33

## Do People Wear Clothes in Heaven?

Adam and Eve were naked in the garden of Eden. My kids wanted to know if that would be the case in heaven. Oh, the horror! Just kidding! That was their reaction to the idea, though. Adam and Eve did not notice their nakedness.

> Now the man and the wife were both naked, but they felt no shame. (Genesis 2:25)

Then, they ate from the tree of good and evil, and they suddenly became aware of their nakedness. God gave them clothes to wear for protection and comfort. There are people in this world who live in nudist colonies where they walk around naked all the time. It does not bother them. The rest of us, though, might be a bit embarrassed to witness or be a part of that. In heaven, if we are naked, we will feel no shame.

However, the Bible does mention clothes. When Jesus appeared in His resurrected body, He was not naked. Also, when John saw Jesus in His heavenly form, Jesus was wearing clothes. When we get to heaven, the Bible compares us, and our clothing, to a bride.

> She has been given the finest of pure white linen to wear. For the fine linen represents the good deeds of God's holy people. (Revelation 19:8)

The white also is significant because it represents righteousness and purity. We will no longer feel the shame of our sinful nature. We will be made new.

All who are victorious will be clothed in white. I will never erase their names from the Book of Life, but I will announce before my Father and his angels that they are mine. (Revelation 3:5)

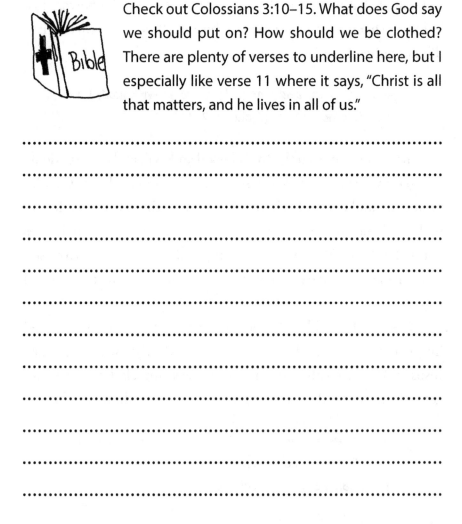

Check out Colossians 3:10–15. What does God say we should put on? How should we be clothed? There are plenty of verses to underline here, but I especially like verse 11 where it says, "Christ is all that matters, and he lives in all of us."

# 34

## Can You Get Sick in Heaven?

Sickness is caused by bad bacteria, viruses, and even the body attacking itself. These are all results of *the fall* when Adam and Eve sinned. Our new bodies will not get sick thanks to what Jesus did for us.

> But he was pierced for our rebellion, crushed for our sins. He was beaten so we could be whole. He was whipped so we could be healed. (Isaiah 53:5)

We will live forever without our bodies declining or weakening. There will be no more sniffles and coughs. There will be no more life-threatening illnesses.

It can be hard to watch people get seriously ill. These past few years, many people have died from viruses like Covid-19. We prayed for a lot of people who thankfully recovered. We also prayed for people who did not get well. When we pray for healing, sometimes God's answer is to heal a person in this life. However, sometimes His answer is to heal them in heaven. That is hard! I prayed for my mom to be healed from her disease, but God chose instead to take her home to be with Him. She loved Jesus and trusted in His perfect plan for her. I am so glad she is healed now, and that she will be there when God calls me home. Her illness drew me even closer to my Great Comforter. Still, losing people we love is hard. I am so thankful there is no sickness in heaven!

Have you had to say goodbye to someone because of illness? Are you, or someone you know, praying for healing? How does knowing there is no sickness in heaven make you feel?

...............................................................................

...............................................................................

...............................................................................

...............................................................................

...............................................................................

...............................................................................

...............................................................................

...............................................................................

...............................................................................

...............................................................................

...............................................................................

Thank you, Jesus, for dying on a cross so we could be made new and be restored. It is hard to be sick, or to watch others go through difficult illnesses. It is even harder when people die from diseases. Please help us trust You during times of sickness and health. When we pray for healing, sometimes Your answer is "yes" in this life, but sometimes it is "yes" in heaven in a resurrected body. Please help us to be patient for whichever healing You provide. Thank you for Your gift of life forever with You! In Your precious name we pray, Amen!

# 35

## Are You Endlessly Happy in Heaven?

**Won't we be sad if some of our friends and family are not there with us?**

> Look! I am creating new heavens and a new earth,
> and no one will even think about the old ones anymore.
> (Isaiah 65:17)

 This is a tough question because the Bible tells us there will be no sadness in heaven. Yet, how can we not grieve those who reject Jesus and face the consequences of that? What if we think about it this way?

You are sitting in your classroom and the teacher says she has a fabulous ice cream party planned for recess, and *all you must do to attend is to ask her to sign you up by adding your name to the guest list.* Those who fail to sign up will spend their recess cleaning bathrooms. Some ask immediately to be signed up. Some need a few reminders and warnings that they are going to miss out, but they too ensure their names are on the party list.

Still, there are kids, including your best friend, who refuse to sign up. They poke fun at the requirement of signing up, mock the teacher, question if there really will be ice cream, and attempt to distract those around them. You feel a bit anxious about your friend and are frustrated by the disobedience. You try to convince your friend to just listen to the teacher. You have been looking forward to enjoying recess together.

Over and over the teacher gives more chances. Finally, the bell rings, signaling the end of the class period. It is time for recess. You race outside with a bunch of other friends and sit down with your delicious ice cream. You momentarily think of your friend back in the classroom facing the consequence of rejecting the teacher's instructions. You wish that friend had chosen differently, but you are now focused on the friends all around you and the incredible party for those of you who accepted the invitation.

> He will wipe every tear from their eyes, and there will be no more death or sorrow or crying or pain. All these things are gone forever. (Revelation 21:4)

Thankfully we will not feel sadness in heaven, but hopefully you do feel a sense of urgency right now to share Jesus with your friends, family, and strangers too. Everyone needs Jesus before it is too late.

Check out 2 Peter 3:3–15. Who in your life needs to hear about Jesus? Ask God to present you with an opportunity to share about your faith. How do you feel about verse 9? I think it is a good verse to underline!

......................................................................

......................................................................

......................................................................

......................................................................

......................................................................

......................................................................

......................................................................

......................................................................

......................................................................

......................................................................

......................................................................

......................................................................

......................................................................

......................................................................

......................................................................

......................................................................

......................................................................

......................................................................

......................................................................

......................................................................

......................................................................

......................................................................

Heavenly Father, thanks for Your patience as You wait for as many people as possible to repent. Please give me the words I need to share Your truth with others. Please give me opportunities to share why my faith is so important to me. Please help me to be brave and to ask others to come with me to Sunday school or to church events. Thank you, God, for Your faithfulness and grace. In Jesus's name I pray. Amen!

# 36

## Will There Be Rich and Poor People in Heaven?

What do you think it means to be rich? What is your own definition? Some might say it means having lots of money. Others might say it means having lots of stuff. A few might even say richness determines how good life is. If they are healthy, safe, and have a family, they are rich. What do you think? Just for fun, let's play a round of *Would You Rather.*

> Would you rather have an unlimited source of money, but be sick all the time; or would you rather be healthy, but have no money?
>
> Would you rather be surrounded by people who love you and support you, but not be able to buy any video game systems or toys; or would you rather be rich and famous, owning everything you've ever dreamed of, but be surrounded by people who like you only for your money and fame?

The Bible has some things to say about wealth, riches, and priorities.

> In that day he will be your sure foundation, providing a rich store of salvation, wisdom, and knowledge. The fear of the Lord will be your treasure. (Isaiah 33:6)

What if we define "rich" in terms of our salvation and hope in Jesus? There is a man in Matthew 19 who asks Jesus a question. He wants to know what he must do to inherit eternal life. Jesus tells him to obey the commandments, like love your neighbor as yourself. The man insists he does this, so Jesus challenges him to sell all he has and give it to the poor so he can have treasures in heaven. He then invites the man to follow Him. The problem is the rich man values his riches, and the security they bring him, more than he values heaven. He is unable to trust Jesus. He walks away sad because he is not prepared to give up everything to follow Jesus.

> And everyone who has given up houses or brothers or sisters or father or mother or children or property, for my sake, will receive a hundred times as much in return and will inherit eternal life. (Matthew 19:29)

What does this mean? If we trust Jesus with our lives, and we obey Him no matter what He asks of us, we will be rich both here and in heaven. However, it is important to know that we won't necessarily be rich in health, wealth, or any other things we might hope for. Instead, we will be rich in the truth that we will spend forever with God after serving Him well. Even if we had no money, no family, poor health, and no home, we would have God, and He is enough.

This world has people who are poor in "stuff" but rich in faith. It has people who are rich in "stuff" but poor in faith. In this broken world, people go hungry and suffer from health problems. Our new world will not be broken, and people will not be poor. Everyone will experience the richness of God's grace and love. Everyone will have everything they need and more. There will be no rich and poor in heaven. We all will be richer than rich!

 Underline 2 Corinthians 4:16–18 in your Bible. It is worth remembering!

Jesus, thank you that when we fix our eyes on You, we can be renewed every day. Help us see that our current worries and troubles will not last forever. We have life with You to look forward to. What a reward that is! Amen!

# 37

## What Language Will We Speak in Heaven?

Hola! Bonjour! Hallo!

We certainly speak a lot of languages. We can thank the people of Babel for that! So, which one do we get to speak in heaven? It's a fair question.

I do not know if we all will learn one language; if we will automatically know a common language; or if it will be like it was at a celebration called Pentecost nearly two months after Jesus had been crucified. Listen to what happened to all the believers gathered there in Acts 2.

Then, what looked like flames or tongues of fire appeared and settled on each of them. And everyone present was filled with the Holy Spirit and began speaking in other languages, as the Holy Spirit gave them this ability.

At that time there were devout Jews from every nation living in Jerusalem. When they heard the loud noise, everyone came running, and they were bewildered to hear their own languages being spoken by the believers.

They were completely amazed. "How can this be?" they exclaimed. "These people are all from Galilee, and yet we hear them speaking in our own native languages!" (Acts 2:3-8)

These believers from all over could understand each other through the power of the Holy Spirit!

What do you think now about language in heaven? God certainly gave us an amazing example of what He *could* have planned for us one day. We will have to wait and see. In the meantime, how might you communicate the love of Jesus to someone who does not speak English? Sometimes actions speak louder than words. What are some ways you could share Jesus with someone without having to use words?

I have a friend who is a missionary in a place where the people do not have a Bible in their own language. Her family moved to this country to learn the language and translate the Bible for these people. While her family is studying the language, they also are serving and loving their neighbors. Most importantly, they are building relationships with people, because when it comes to sharing Jesus, words are not always necessary.

Have you ever visited with kids from other countries? My parents joked that when I was a kid, every time I met a person who did not speak English, it was like I could understand their language and they could understand me, even though I had no idea how to speak anything but English. No translation is needed for a smile, enthusiasm, kindness, understanding, or even a hug.

I did not know Jesus back then, but once I committed my life to God, I wanted to learn another language so I could communicate the love of Jesus not only in actions, but also in words.

> What about you? What are some ways you can communicate God's love to others, whether through words or actions?

Place a checkmark next to ideas you might try.

➢ Learn a few friendly greetings in another language.
➢ Make cookies and deliver them to someone with a smile.
➢ Choose a local service project to do with your family.
➢ Write a note of encouragement to someone.
➢ Welcome a new neighbor, or greet a new kid at school.
➢ Read a book to a younger child.
➢ Help greet kids as they arrive to Sunday school.
➢ Pray for Christians in other countries, especially those in countries where it is illegal or discouraged to worship Jesus.
➢ Other _____

Check out Psalm 19:1–4. How far is God's truth able to spread and be understood? Who helped you, in words or actions, to understand God's love for you?

...........................................................
...........................................................
...........................................................
...........................................................
...........................................................
...........................................................

# 38

## Does Time Stand Still in Heaven?

Time is such an interesting concept. God already knows what will happen in the future, and He was there before "in the beginning" happened. God exists outside of time.

So, what does the Bible say about time and what God can do with it?

Did you know God made a sundial (or ancient clock) move backward?

> I will cause the sun's shadow to move ten steps backward on the sundial of Ahaz!'" So the shadow on the sundial moved backward ten steps. (Isaiah 38:8)

I don't know about you, but I have never seen the sun reverse course, so that is impressive. The Bible also says this about time.

> But you must not forget this one thing, dear friends: A day is like a thousand years to the Lord, and a thousand years is like a day. (2 Peter 3:8)

This verse could mean that in eternity, time does not really matter. What might feel like one day in heaven could be like 1,000 years in our world. Either way, it is not going to matter in the way time matters to us now. Every year, as we get older here in this life, we are aging. When we no longer age in heaven, then keeping track of the years no longer matters.

Because we know from the Bible that God has always existed, even before the creation of the universe, and we know He has the power to do anything, we really cannot begin to grasp God's relationship with time as we know it. We know that God views time differently than we do. We also know that in heaven, time will go on forever—for eternity. Forever is a really hard thing for us to understand when a day, week, or year, can seem like a long time! Have you ever heard the saying, "Time flies when you are having fun?" I imagine we will feel that way in heaven.

God is all powerful, and if He wants to stop time, reverse time, or even step outside of time, He is able. Will time stop in heaven? I guess it depends if anyone bothers to ask, "What time is it?" or if anyone pauses from having fun to measure that passing time.

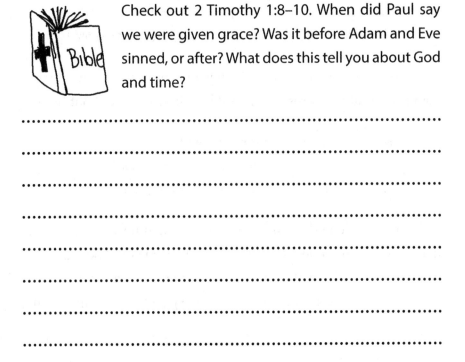

Check out 2 Timothy 1:8–10. When did Paul say we were given grace? Was it before Adam and Eve sinned, or after? What does this tell you about God and time?

. . . . . . . . . . . . . . . . . . . . . . . . . . . . . . . . . . . . . . . . . . . . . . . . . . . . . . . .

. . . . . . . . . . . . . . . . . . . . . . . . . . . . . . . . . . . . . . . . . . . . . . . . . . . . . . . .

. . . . . . . . . . . . . . . . . . . . . . . . . . . . . . . . . . . . . . . . . . . . . . . . . . . . . . . .

. . . . . . . . . . . . . . . . . . . . . . . . . . . . . . . . . . . . . . . . . . . . . . . . . . . . . . . .

. . . . . . . . . . . . . . . . . . . . . . . . . . . . . . . . . . . . . . . . . . . . . . . . . . . . . . . .

. . . . . . . . . . . . . . . . . . . . . . . . . . . . . . . . . . . . . . . . . . . . . . . . . . . . . . . .

. . . . . . . . . . . . . . . . . . . . . . . . . . . . . . . . . . . . . . . . . . . . . . . . . . . . . . . .

Thank you, Jesus, that You knew we would need grace before You ever created us, so You planned from the beginning to save us. Just like You gave Adam and Eve a choice by placing the Tree of Life in the Garden of Eden, You give us a choice to accept Your gift of forgiveness. Nothing surprises You. You know everything, and we thank You that forever is a very long time. Amen!

Can you solve these riddles?

1. How many months have 28 days?
2. I am the beginning of the end, as well as the end of time and space. I am essential to creation, and I surround every place. What am I?
3. What comes once in a minute, twice in a moment, but never in a thousand years?

1. All of them. 2. The letter "e." 3. The letter "m."
Source https://www.riddles.nu/topics/time

# 39

## Will People Know Who You Are?
### Like Would George Washington Know Who I Am?

Hebrews 11 is a fascinating chapter of the Bible to read. It is a list of Bible heroes who had faith that inspires us thousands of years later. We know about what they did because it was recorded in the pages of scripture. So, when you meet Noah, Moses, Abraham, Rahab, and Ruth, to name a few, you will know them. You will know a part of their story. Imagine how exciting it will be walking around one day, and suddenly you run into Mary, Paul, or David! I know I sure would like to sit down and talk with many of the people we meet on the pages of the Bible.

> Therefore, since we are surrounded by such a huge crowd of witnesses to the life of faith, let us strip off every weight that slows us down, especially the sin that so easily trips us up. And let us run with endurance the race God has set before us. We do this by keeping our eyes on Jesus, the champion who initiates and perfects our faith. Because of the joy awaiting him, he endured the cross, disregarding its shame. Now he is seated in the place of honor beside God's throne. (Hebrews 12: 1–2)

In the same way that these ancient people inspire you, you might be inspired by people from modern history as well. I do not know if George Washington will recognize you as you recognize him, but I do know there will be *plenty* of people who recognize you. Perhaps some of them will have looked to you as a hero of faith—someone who pointed them to Jesus. Perhaps some of them will have observed your life and will be looking forward to meeting you and hearing more about your story.

In John 20, Mary Magdalene was crying outside the tomb of Jesus. Some angels asked her why she was crying. She did not recognize them as angels, nor did she recognize Jesus.

> She turned to leave and saw someone standing there. It was Jesus, but she didn't recognize him. "Dear woman, why are you crying?" Jesus asked her. "Who are you looking for?"
>
> She thought he was the gardener. "Sir," she said, "if you have taken him away, tell me where you have put him, and I will go and get him."
>
> "Mary!" Jesus said.
>
> She turned to him and cried out, "Rabboni!" (which is Hebrew for "Teacher").
>
> "Don't cling to me," Jesus said, "For I haven't yet ascended to the Father. But go find my brothers and tell them, 'I am ascending to my Father and your Father, to my God and your God.'" (John 20:14–17)

Have you ever run into someone familiar in a setting completely unexpected? For example, what if while on vacation you ran into your dentist or a kid from school? You might be so surprised to see them there, you might not recognize them at first. Mary was not looking for a living Jesus. It did not even cross her mind that Jesus could be standing right there. I wonder if this means Jesus looked a little bit different than normal, or if it was just her grief and confusion causing her to miss his presence. Either way, she recognized Him immediately when He called her by name.

One day, He will call you by name!

Even though we all will be getting new bodies—the best versions of ourselves—our personalities will shine as brightly as our outer appearances. I imagine we will be quite recognizable to those who know us best. If we have never met someone before, I doubt it will take long to form a connection. Maybe we will discover we know someone in common, have a similar life experience, or share the same interests. We will be brothers and sisters in Christ, which means we will be family and share a family tree. We will have all the time we need to get to know one another.

Who would you most like to meet when
you get to heaven? Make a list below! Then,
check out the fun Bible personality quiz!

...............................................................................

...............................................................................

...............................................................................

...............................................................................

...............................................................................

...............................................................................

...............................................................................

# To which Bible hero do you most relate?

1.  **When God asks you to do something difficult for Him, your first instinct is to ...**
    A.  Ask Him to choose someone else.
    B.  Think of others first, even if it means leaving your comfort zone.
    C.  Get it done quickly, implementing a wise plan using the tools He has given you.
    D.  Pray about it and seek His direction.

2.  **God just put you in charge of a situation. What do you do?**
    A.  Rely on others to speak for you or with you as you work as a team.
    B.  Protect and stick close to those you love, even if it means missing out on something you might want to do more.
    C.  Calmly direct others and negotiate to accomplish your goal.
    D.  Call on the Holy Spirit to help you educate those around you as you share truth.

3.  **If God gave you a Holy Spirit superpower, you would be most excited to ...**
    A.  Make your enemies' lives miserable enough that they believe God is real.
    B.  Persuade someone to go along with your plan and trust you.
    C.  Stop a war from happening.
    D.  Perform miracles.

4.  **If you could be known for just one thing, it would be ...**
    A.  Your leadership.
    B.  Your faithfulness.
    C.  Your wisdom.
    D.  Your evangelism (How you tell others about Jesus).

**5. To which fear do you most relate?**

A. Public speaking

B. Rejection (not being wanted)

C. People making bad choices

D. Large groups of angry people

Which letter did you pick most often? Add up your choices. (It's Ok if it was a tie.) Have fun reading your results.

_____ A          _____ C

_____ B          _____ D

If you chose mostly **A,** you are like Moses. He had some doubts about his abilities, but with God's help, and the help of his brother, he called down plagues on the Egyptians. He convinced the Israelites to flee with him, experienced God on a mountain top, and became one of the greatest leaders of all time.

If you chose mostly **B,** you are like Ruth from the book of Ruth. She faced a difficult choice when her husband died, but instead of going back to her original family, she followed her mother-in-law to keep her company in her sadness, take care of her, and provide for her needs in a time when women without husbands or sons faced many difficulties. She worked hard to find food and overcame her fears to persuade a good man to marry her.

If you chose mostly **C,** you are like Abigail, King David's wife from 1 Samuel 25. Abigail's husband at the time cheated David and insulted him. David was about to take his revenge, but Abigail thought fast, organized her servants, and met David and his mighty men with gifts, apologies, and a convincing argument about why

David should not sin by attacking her household. David agreed and praised her good judgment. God struck Abigail's husband dead less than two weeks afterward, and David offered to marry Abigail.

If you chose mostly **D**, you are like Paul. A brilliant student and Jewish leader, he was making a name for himself by killing Christians. He wanted success and honor from other religious leaders. Then, he became a Christ follower and was forgiven for his sins. He made known the name of Jesus instead of making a name for himself. Through the power of the Holy Spirit, he did God's work, teaching truth, encouraging believers, performing miracles, and standing strong when persecuted for his faith and obedience to the one true King.

Who are some other Bible personalities you can relate to? How are you similar to these real people from history?

...............................................................................

...............................................................................

...............................................................................

...............................................................................

...............................................................................

...............................................................................

...............................................................................

...............................................................................

...............................................................................

...............................................................................

...............................................................................

# 40

## Will There Be Aliens in Heaven?

Assuming we are talking about "aliens" like we picture creatures from outer space, then this is going to have to remain a mystery. However, the Bible does talk about human aliens. The word alien means anyone who is not part of your group, country, or world. So, guess what? We all are "aliens" of this world. Our identity and home is with Christ.

> For this world is not our permanent home; we are looking forward to a home yet to come. (Hebrews 13:14)

> So now you Gentiles are no longer strangers and foreigners. You are citizens along with all of God's holy people. You are members of God's family. Together, we are his house, built on the foundation of the apostles and the prophets. And the cornerstone is Christ Jesus himself. We are carefully joined together in him, becoming a holy temple for the Lord. Through him you Gentiles are also being made part of this dwelling where God lives by his Spirit. (Ephesians 2:19–22)

No matter where we come from, or with whom we share DNA, we are all adopted into God's family. This means we belong to the King of Kings. We are royalty.

Check out Colossians 4:5-6. Knowing that we all are aliens, or foreigners of this world, how does God want us to live? How do your conversations reflect Jesus? Are your words gracious and attractive? If not, how might these verses be challenging you?

...................................................................

...................................................................

...................................................................

...................................................................

...................................................................

...................................................................

...................................................................

...................................................................

...................................................................

...................................................................

...................................................................

...................................................................

...................................................................

...................................................................

...................................................................

...................................................................

...................................................................

...................................................................

# 41

## Do We Still Go to School in Heaven? Do We Go to Sunday School?

*Heaven School by Eagan, 12*

Some of us love school—others, not so much. My kids and their friends were chatting in the car one day about school. One boy said he disliked all things about school except, perhaps, if you count lunch and recess. My son would be happy to study history all day. My daughter would prefer gym class. My husband loved school so much, he wished he could be a student forever. So, if there is no pain or sadness in heaven, does that mean our friend would get endless recess, my husband would be given science experiments, my son would read history books, and my daughter would get to do gymnastics all day?

And, what about Sunday school? You all know I love to teach my Sunday school friends, but can you imagine me teaching you all about Jesus with Jesus sitting in the room with us? That would be silly! I think I would happily sit and listen to Jesus teach forever!

The Bible does not say for sure, but there is no reason to think we would stop learning and growing in heaven. There are still so many things we have not yet learned. I certainly have questions and there are many things I wonder. I hope there is a school of sorts. If there are flying classes with the angels, my daughter and I would be the first to sign up!

What do you think? I think we will all enjoy learning more about our Creator. We will not need a building and desks to learn. We will not be graded. We will simply enjoy having the Almighty— the source of all knowledge—as our Leader, Teacher, and Father.

In the meantime, for those of us who have received God's gracious gift and are adopted into His forever family, we have the Holy Spirit teaching us all the time! Because of the Holy Spirit, we can know God. Our hearts are changed when we accept Him as our Lord and Savior, and He helps us understand what God's Word means. He helps us understand truth.

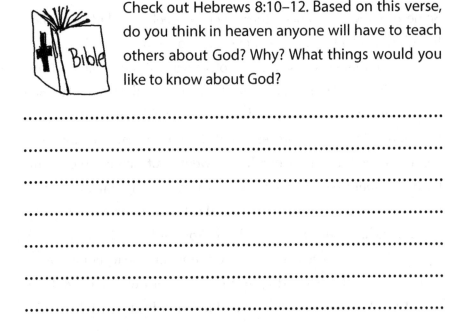

Check out Hebrews 8:10–12. Based on this verse, do you think in heaven anyone will have to teach others about God? Why? What things would you like to know about God?

· · · · · · · · · · · · · · · · · · · · · · · · · · · · · · · · · · · · · · · · · · · · · · · · · · · · · ·

· · · · · · · · · · · · · · · · · · · · · · · · · · · · · · · · · · · · · · · · · · · · · · · · · · · · · ·

· · · · · · · · · · · · · · · · · · · · · · · · · · · · · · · · · · · · · · · · · · · · · · · · · · · · · ·

· · · · · · · · · · · · · · · · · · · · · · · · · · · · · · · · · · · · · · · · · · · · · · · · · · · · · ·

· · · · · · · · · · · · · · · · · · · · · · · · · · · · · · · · · · · · · · · · · · · · · · · · · · · · · ·

· · · · · · · · · · · · · · · · · · · · · · · · · · · · · · · · · · · · · · · · · · · · · · · · · · · · · ·

· · · · · · · · · · · · · · · · · · · · · · · · · · · · · · · · · · · · · · · · · · · · · · · · · · · · · ·

# 42

## Do You Get to Live with Your Family in Heaven?

Have you ever seen a family tree? My mom made me a baby book full of photos from when I was a child. In it was a drawing of a tree, and it had spaces for all the names of my family members like my grandparents, aunts, uncles, brothers, sisters, and cousins. These people were all connected to me either by DNA (our genes) or by marriage. Some kids may not share genetic connections with their family, but they share the connection of belonging to people who love them.

The word family means something different to everyone. Some people have small families. Others have big families. Some people do not have families, but they have good friends they consider family. While some of you might have positive thoughts about your family, some of you might feel like people in your family have let you down or hurt you. Not everyone is able to think about family and feel loved. I have a friend who used to belong to a different religion. In her religion, some people hate Christians. When she became a Christian, her family told her they no longer loved her, and she was told to leave and never come back. Her children do not know their grandparents, aunts, uncles, and cousins. They had to leave them all behind to follow Jesus.

So, then who is our family?

> As Jesus was speaking to the crowd, his mother and brothers stood outside, asking to speak to him. Someone told Jesus, "Your mother and your brothers are standing outside, and they want to speak to you."
>
> Jesus asked, "Who is my mother? Who are my brothers?" Then he pointed to his disciples and said, "Look, these are my mother and brothers. Anyone who does the will of my Father in heaven is my brother and sister and mother!" (Matthew 12:46–50)

Jesus was born fully God and fully man. His father is God. His mother, Mary, shared DNA with Jesus, and that is why Jesus also was human. He had half brothers and sisters. He had uncles, aunts, and grandparents. Even though those people claimed Jesus as part of their DNA—their blood—it was His blood that gave us all life when He died on the cross. Jesus was not being disrespectful to His family when they asked to see Him. He wanted to make sure they, and everyone listening, knew that His family includes all of us.

In summary...

**Q: Will we get to live with our family in heaven?**

A: If we are thinking of family as including all believers in Jesus—your brothers and sisters in Christ—then yes. You will live with your family.

**Q: Will your earthly family members be there?**

A: If they know Jesus, and trust Him as their Savior, they will be there too.

Q: Will you share the same living space?

A: We can wonder, but God says He is preparing a place for you, so whatever that looks like, it will be exactly what you need and exactly where you need to be. And, if your family enjoys eating meals together, the good news is we all will be seated at the table with Jesus. Nobody will be left out!

Do you go to church? If you do, then you have a church family. Church is a place where we can come together with other believers to build each other up before heading back into the world. It is the place where we worship God together, just like we will one day in heaven. It is the place where we serve each other and use the gifts God gave us. It is so important for us to spend time with other brothers and sisters in Christ and encourage each other.

Do you know anybody who believes in Jesus like you do? List some names below and think of ways you can encourage that brother or sister in Christ. Make another list of people that you hope will join your forever family, and make sure to pray for them.

My Forever Family.

People I am praying will join God's family.

*By Ivy, 12*

# 43

## Will We Be Able to Recognize Each Other in Our New Bodies?

Have you ever run into someone and wondered, "Where have I seen you before? You look *so* familiar!" That happens to me sometimes. I also am terrible at remembering names. I used to be good with remembering faces, but the older I get, the worse my memory is. Thank goodness I will have a new body and restored mind in heaven! I hope that means my brain will be amazing at remembering names, because otherwise God will need to provide all of us with name tags, just for me. (Or maybe for you too?)

If we are getting new bodies in heaven, it is fair to wonder if we will look very different, and if friends and family would be able to recognize us. We often rely on human senses to gather information—especially sight. Sometimes we even make judgments about a person based on what we see.

"...People judge by outward appearance, but the Lord looks at the heart." (1 Samuel 16:7)

Even children are known by the way they act, whether their conduct is pure, and whether it is right. (Proverbs 20:11)

We can't see someone's heart, but can we know someone without seeing them? If you walked into a completely dark room with all your friends, would you be able to recognize anybody? We could be resourceful and use senses other than our sight, right?

**Like Smell!** You might be able to recognize a few people by scent—their shampoo, detergent on their clothes, food smells, and when they forget to wear deodorant. Can anyone relate to that last one? But, let's pretend for a minute that we *are* bathing/showering in heaven, and that nobody would stink. I guess smell might not be the best first clue.

**How about touch?** I suppose you could try feeling someone's hair, or the shape of their nose. However, we likely will all look a bit different if our bodies will be perfect, so this might not be a good strategy either. Plus, that would be kind of awkward.

**What about sound?** I can recognize the kids in my classroom by the sounds of their voices. How about you? Could you recognize a voice or two or three? Jesus recognizes our voices.

My sheep listen to my voice; I know them, and they follow me. (John 10:27)

We will recognize a very important voice—that of Jesus. So, recognizing voices could be a good strategy—especially if people are calling us by name! Thankfully, heaven won't be dark, and we will be able to see.

All that to say, you will recognize people. Just like when I see those people I can't quite place, after a quick conversation, my memory kicks in and I usually remember how I know the person, or we both recall a past interaction. Sometimes we become friends anyway after exhausting all our, "Do I know you from..." lists.

God created us to live in community with each other. When you love someone, you would recognize them anywhere. Even people we don't know well will feel familiar. Do you ever get the feeling like you have met someone before? Everyone we meet might just feel familiar like that, because we all will be brothers and sisters in Christ. *We will recognize Jesus in each other!* Once we have a chance to talk and share and laugh together, I have a feeling we will recognize people without needing name tags!

If God looks at your heart (meaning who you are as a person, and not the way you look) what beautiful things does He see? Circle or put a heart around traits God sees in you. Can you add more to the list?

| | | |
|---|---|---|
| Friendly | Joyful | Faithful |
| Kind | Fair | Generous |
| Gentle | Just | Courageous |
| Peaceful | Helpful | Thoughtful |
| Loving | Giving | Curious |

Dear Jesus, we thank You that when we choose You, we receive the Holy Spirit to help us be beautiful on the inside. Because You died on a cross for us, we are no longer ugly with sin. You know us and recognize us as Your beautiful children. We love You! Amen!

# 44

## With So Many People, How Will You See Them All?

You know, this is a great question for an extrovert! An extrovert is someone who feels energized around other people. Others are introverts. They still like people, but they re-energize while spending time alone. God created both kinds of personalities.

As an extrovert, I feel like I will want to see *everyone*, and probably as soon as possible. An introvert might feel like there is plenty of time and may need some "people breaks." It is a good thing our amazing God has promised us a gorgeously restored new earth to enjoy in occasional peaceful solitude (alone) if we need that, and with our huge forever family.

So, to answer the question, you will have eternity to meet every single person in heaven. Eternity means time never runs out. You literally have forever to hang out with people, or to chill out by yourself.

 Check out 1 Peter 5:7. What worries you about the future, or about what things might be like in heaven? What does God tell you to do about those worries? Write a prayer below and give your worries to God.

....................................................................

....................................................................

# 45

## What If Your Family is Not in Heaven?

Who do you consider your favorite people? Do you have a cousin you love like a brother or sister? Do you enjoy your aunts, uncles, grandparents, parents, and family friends who are around so much that they might as well be family? Maybe you do not have connection to relatives who share your DNA, but perhaps you have a family that God has provided through love.

No matter who you love to spend time with most, all of us could agree that we like to enjoy new experiences with our favorite people. We like to go to new places knowing a familiar face or two. It is tough to go somewhere unfamiliar and not have our caregivers there to support us. We rely on those who take care of us to lead us and guide us.

We know some fabulous things about heaven, though!

1. First, you have a Father in heaven who loves you and cares for all your needs. You have a best friend in Jesus who leads and guides you. You have the Holy Spirit who is with you always.

2. Second, heaven will feel like a familiar place, because it will be the home you might not even realize you have been missing so much.

3. Third, heaven is a safe place with no danger, sadness, pain, suffering, or loneliness. You literally cannot be unhappy

there, no matter the order you and your family members and friends arrive.

The cool thing about heaven is that even if you were the only person there with God, you would still feel complete. Thankfully, it will not be just you and God. You will be surrounded by a huge family of brothers and sisters in Christ, as well as angels, who care about you. Everyone will live in peace and love.

In Hebrews 13:5 God promises never to leave us or abandon us. That makes me know He would not let me feel abandoned in heaven. I also know He loves us and promises to take care of us.

> And this same God who takes care of me will supply all your needs from his glorious riches, which have been given to us in Christ Jesus. (Philippians 4:19)

The Bible tells us that God has made us into one family, or body of believers, with Him as the head leader. Together, we will grow in love now and in heaven. Never forget how much God loves you.

> Instead, we will speak the truth in love, growing in every way more and more like Christ, who is the head of his body, the church. He makes the whole body fit together perfectly. As each part does its own special work, it helps the other parts grow, so that the whole body is healthy and growing and full of love. (Ephesians 4:15–16)

> Then Christ will make his home in your hearts as you trust in him. Your roots will grow down into God's love and keep you strong. And may you have the power to understand, as all God's people should, how wide, how

long, how high, and how deep his love is. May you experience the love of Christ, though it is too great to understand fully. Then you will be made complete with all the fullness of life and power that comes from God. Now all glory to God, who is able, through his mighty power at work within us, to accomplish infinitely more than we might ask or think. (Ephesians 3:17–20)

Check out Philippians 4:4–7. Does God want us to worry? What does God promise us? What are some of your worries you can share with God? Don't be afraid to tell Him!

........................................................................

........................................................................

........................................................................

........................................................................

........................................................................

........................................................................

........................................................................

........................................................................

........................................................................

........................................................................

........................................................................

........................................................................

# 46

## If We Want Something, Will It Just Show up as Soon as We Imagine It?

Well, to answer this, I think we should look at a passage in the book of Matthew.

> Keep on asking, and you will receive what you ask for. Keep on seeking, and you will find. Keep on knocking, and the door will be opened to you. For everyone who asks, receives. Everyone who seeks, finds. And to everyone who knocks, the door will be opened. (Matthew 7:7–8)

So, does this mean God is like a magic genie ready to grant you every wish you have? Not to burst any bubbles, but I am going to have to say, nope. This verse means that when we are following God's plan, He will answer our prayers and give us help to accomplish His work. It means His door is never closed to us. We can approach Him with our requests. It also means that anyone who asks to be part of His family—who seeks Him—will find Him.

God knows your needs, and He provides for them. He knows the desires of your heart before you even know them.

> Take delight in the LORD, and he will give you your heart's desires. (Psalm 37:4)

Let us just think for a moment, though. Is everything you want right now good for you? I would like to eat a bunch of brownies with some ice cream on top. However, that is not good for me. Part of God taking care of us means sometimes He gives us a "no" answer.

Now, perhaps our perfect bodies in heaven will allow us to eat all the brownies and ice cream we want, and perhaps dessert will appear every time we think of it. I do not know, but I do know that God has a plan for us, even in heaven, and God knows what is best for us. He will delight us, provide for us, and maybe even surprise us with a few "poof, there it is" moments.

It is important for us to remember that our purpose is to serve and glorify (worship) God. I have a feeling God will be delighting us with the desires of our hearts more than we can possibly imagine, but the desires of our hearts probably will not be for "stuff." I tend to think my greatest desire will be to love and adore my King of Kings. I will want to spend time with Him more than anything or anyone else.

 Check out Ephesians 3:18–21. What do you think it means that you will be made complete by God? How much does Jesus love you? How does knowing that affect the desires of your heart? What do you desire, or want, from God?

.......................................................................

.......................................................................

.......................................................................

.......................................................................

.......................................................................

........................................................................

........................................................................

........................................................................

........................................................................

........................................................................

........................................................................

........................................................................

........................................................................

........................................................................

........................................................................

Thank you, Heavenly Father, for loving us so much that You delight in us. Thank you that You give us everything we need to serve You, and thanks for the great plans You have for us here and in heaven. Please help us to trust You when You tell us You have prepared a place for us in heaven. Even though we cannot see that place right now, we know You always do what You say You will do. We also know that it will be more amazing than we could possibly imagine. Thanks for giving us an imagination to dream about heaven. Help us to look forward to that day with excitement and anticipation, but also to remain focused on the jobs You give us now, like loving our neighbors and sharing Your truth with them. In Jesus's name we pray. Amen!

# 47

## Do We Celebrate Things Like Birthdays and Christmas?

If we look at examples in the Bible, it seems to me that God loves a good celebration. In the Old Testament book of Leviticus, God gave a *lot* of instructions to His people. Those instructions included hosting feasts and festivals. They observed these for many reasons including the following:

1. To remind people what God had done and would do for them.
2. To honor God for providing for His people.
3. To practice obedience in following God's instructions.
4. To encourage God's people to gather.

---

True or False: These are the festivals and feasts that God instructs his people to celebrate in Leviticus 23.

1. _____ The Passover
2. _____ Feast of First Vegetables
3. _____ Feast of First Fruits
4. _____ Feast of Weeks
5. _____ Feast of Months
6. _____ Feast of Drums
7. _____ Feast of Trumpets
8. _____ Feast of Tabernacles
9. _____ Day of Atonement

Answers: 1. T, 2. F, 3. T, 4. T, 5. F, 6. F, 7. T, 8. T, 9. T.

---

God wants people to celebrate. Even myriads (a whole bunch) of angels celebrate in heaven.

> All heaven will praise your great wonders, LORD; myriads of angels will praise you for your faithfulness. (Psalm 89:5)

God did not command us to celebrate the birth of Jesus, but we do that when we gather on Christmas Eve or Christmas Day. We celebrate that birthday, and we look forward to the return of Jesus. Many of us give gifts as we remember His gift.

What about your birthday? God did not put instructions in the Bible for us to celebrate birthdays, but He does want us to value life and to know we were made for a purpose. He knows every detail about us. Psalm 139:13 says He created you in our mother's womb. He knows everything about you. It says in Luke 12:7 He even knows how many hairs are on your head.

We have already discussed the feast we will one day have in heaven, so I think it is safe to assume we will be doing a lot of celebrating. You will probably find yourself celebrating for all sorts of reasons as you remember what God did for you, and you will praise Him for all He will continue to do for you simply because He loves you so much.

Check out Psalm 108:1-5. How does the writer, King David, feel about praising God? Have you ever felt like praising and celebrating God? What made you feel that way?

· · · · · · · · · · · · · · · · · · · · · · · · · · · · · · · · · · · · · · · · · · · · · · · · · · · · · · · · · ·

· · · · · · · · · · · · · · · · · · · · · · · · · · · · · · · · · · · · · · · · · · · · · · · · · · · · · · · · · ·

· · · · · · · · · · · · · · · · · · · · · · · · · · · · · · · · · · · · · · · · · · · · · · · · · · · · · · · · · ·

# 48

## Do We Wear Uniforms in Heaven?

This is such an interesting question. If you stop for lunch at Chick-fil-A, you will notice workers are wearing a uniform to identify themselves as employees. Similarly, you can recognize police officers and fire fighters by their uniforms. Some of you may wear uniforms to school, and some of you might even have seen people in a church choir wearing matching robes.

Uniforms can make people identifiable, and they can make everyone appear similar. So, will we be wearing uniforms in heaven? Let's think about what we know.

1. God provides for all our needs, so that means He will provide us with clothes if we need them.
2. God loves creativity and beauty, so I imagine these clothes would be lovely.
3. God loves variety. Look at the examples in nature! However, God also likes order, which we can see in areas like mathematics.

No matter what we will be wearing (or not wearing) Revelation 19:8 says we will be clothed in the finest of pure white linen for the wedding feast. This linen also represents the good deeds of God's holy people. So, what does it mean that we will be clothed in white? White, in case you see it in other places in the Bible, can signify purity. It means it has no dirt. Therefore, we will have no sin making us dirty.

> I am overwhelmed with joy in the Lord my God! For he has dressed me with the clothing of salvation and draped me in a robe of righteousness. I am like a bridegroom dressed for his wedding or a bride with her jewels. (Isaiah 61:10)

We will be presented to God as saved and righteous—or right and good. That robe will be like a uniform making us all recognizable as a member of God's family—holy, righteous, and pure.

So, will we wear uniforms in heaven?

Maybe. We certainly will be *uniform* in our appearance of righteousness!

Check out Ephesians 6:10–18. How does God want us to be clothed? It says we should stay alert and pray for believers everywhere. Next time you are in Sunday school, or your regular school, ask your friends how you can pray for them and write their requests below.

..............................................................

..............................................................

..............................................................

..............................................................

..............................................................

..............................................................

..............................................................

# 49

## Could There Ever Be a Time of Total Peace on Earth Where Everybody Can Just Agree?

People sure seem to argue a lot, don't they? This world is full of conflict. Satan loves conflict. He wants nothing more than to keep people so busy fighting and arguing, they will forget about, or ignore God's gift of peace and salvation. Or, even worse, if he can get Christians to fight amongst themselves, he can make people think, "Why would I want to be a Christian, when they are not very nice to each other and they can never seem to agree with each other?"

**POP QUIZ...**

Question: Why can't we all agree and get along?

Answer: Sin

It is as simple as that. Remember that Romans 3:23 says all of us have sinned. We all are imperfect and fall short of God's glorious standard. There are wars. People fight and disagree, and they can be hateful and hurtful. This is the reality of our sinful world. The good news is sin is not forever. Jesus has overcome sin. Meanwhile, Jesus does not leave us without hope or peace.

> I have told you all this so that you may have peace in me. Here on earth you will have many trials and sorrows. But take heart, because I have overcome the world. (John 16:33)

I am leaving you with a gift—peace of mind and heart. And the peace I give is a gift the world cannot give. So don't be troubled or afraid. (John 14:27)

The Bible is clear that there will be people who believe in Jesus, and people who reject Him until the very day of judgment. Jesus will one day judge every heart. Those who choose Him will have peace. Those who reject Him will not.

And anyone whose name was not found recorded in the Book of Life was thrown into the lake of fire. (Revelation 20:15)

This can be upsetting for those of us who have lost family members who did not believe in Jesus. However, we must trust that only God knew their hearts and their choices in the end. Remember the men on the crosses next to Jesus?

One of the criminals hanging beside him scoffed, "So you're the Messiah, are you? Prove it by saving yourself—and us, too, while you're at it!"

But the other criminal protested, "Don't you fear God even when you have been sentenced to die? We deserve to die for our crimes, but this man hasn't done anything wrong." Then he said, "Jesus, remember me when you come into your Kingdom."

And Jesus replied, "I assure you, today you will be with me in paradise." (Luke 23:39-43)

Jesus has the power to save, and we cannot possibly know what occurred in that loved one's heart in the end.

*I am leaving you with a gift—peace of mind and heart. And the peace I give is a gift the world cannot give. So don't be troubled or afraid. (John 14:27)*

Check out Hebrews 4:12–13. Jesus is sometimes referred to as the Word of God, and a Sword. What do you learn about Him from these verses? What does He know about you?

If you want to know more about the final judgment, you can read Revelation 20:10–15. It might be helpful to read this with a parent or trusted adult.

..........................................................................

..........................................................................

..........................................................................

..........................................................................

..........................................................................

..........................................................................

..........................................................................

..........................................................................

..........................................................................

..........................................................................

..........................................................................

..........................................................................

..........................................................................

# 50

## Is There a Sabbath in Heaven?

For those of you wondering what the Sabbath is, let's look quickly back into the Old Testament when God was giving his commandments to the Israelites.

> Remember to observe the Sabbath day by keeping it holy. You have six days each week for your ordinary work, but the seventh day is a Sabbath day of rest dedicated to the Lord your God... (Exodus 20:8-10)

The Sabbath, as defined by God, is a day of rest that is dedicated to honoring Him. Most of us consider this day to be Sunday, but some people designate Saturday as their day of rest.

> So there is a special rest still waiting for the people of God. For all who have entered into God's rest have rested from their labors, just as God did after creating the world. (Hebrews 4:9-10)

The moment we decide to follow Jesus as our Savior and Lord, we find "rest" in Him. It means, we find peace, comfort, strength, but most of all, an assurance of one day spending forever with Him. It does not mean we will live with complete peace and rest on this earth. It just means we can find peace by spending time with Him and trusting Him.

The Sabbath is a day we set aside to spend with God and to rest in Him. When we are in heaven, we will be in the presence of our Mighty God—always! We will forever feel His peace. We will forever experience His "rest." Will there be a special day for us to worship together, like we do with our church family now, or will that happen every day? I do not know, but I hope it is every day! Either way, there will be no shortage of people and angels worshipping God in heaven. There will be no shortage of that feeling of wonder and joy that only comes from the Holy Spirit filling us full to bursting with warmth, peace, and gratefulness.

 Check out Revelation 5:11–14. What is taking place around God's throne, and who is involved?

What is one way you think you might worship God in heaven? Draw a picture or write about it below.

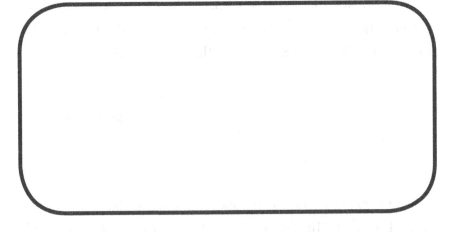

 Will there be a designated day of worship? What do you think as you wonder and imagine the order of our days in heaven?

# 51

## Will You Have a Job in Heaven?

I don't know about you, but I feel pretty good after a day of hard work. I enjoy accomplishing something, and I especially find satisfaction when I am using my gifts to work for God. For example, I love to teach. It brings me so much joy.

What kinds of work do you love?

God has given us each at least one spiritual gift and many talents. Why? He wants us to do work for Him. Serving others is showing them His love. Serving is working for God.

Working hard and doing good will not save us, but our good works are evidence of our faith and the desire to love our neighbors as ourselves. James 2:17 says faith alone is not enough unless it produces good deeds. Otherwise, it is useless. God wants us to have a purpose, and He wants us to work hard at developing the talents He gives us. He does not want us sitting around being lazy. Laziness can lead to boredom and discontent.

> For God is not unjust. He will not forget how hard you have worked for him and how you have shown your love to him by caring for other believers, as you still do. Our great desire is that you will keep on loving others as long as life lasts, in order to make certain that what you hope for will come true. Then you will not become spiritually dull and indifferent. Instead,

you will follow the example of those who are going to inherit God's promises because of their faith and endurance. (Hebrews 6:10–12)

The Bible also says that God rewards us for our faithful work, and it often describes these rewards as crowns.

And now the prize awaits me—the crown of righteousness, which the Lord, the righteous Judge, will give me on the day of his return. And the prize is not just for me but for all who eagerly look forward to his appearing. (2 Timothy 4:8)

While God rewards us in heaven for what we do in our lifetime here, He warns us not to do good to seek attention or try to get something for ourselves. We should not serve God and do good things in hope of earthly rewards—like prizes. But rather, we should think of our rewards in terms of the peace, joy, and satisfaction our work brings. The biggest reward is knowing we will spend forever with God. There is nothing that could top that! No money could buy that. No prize could equal that.

That said, it feels good to be recognized for our work, and God gives rewards for serving Him well. However, these heavenly rewards will not be trophies with which we will line our shelves. We see examples of what we will be doing with these rewards in the book of Revelation.

The twenty-four elders fall down and worship the one sitting on the throne (the one who lives forever and ever). And they lay their crowns before the throne and say, "You are worthy, O Lord our God, to receive glory and honor and power. For you created all things, and they exist because you created what you pleased." (Revelation 4:10-11.)

We do not know for sure who these 24 elders are, but we can expect to follow their example in this situation. We will be given rewards, and we will feel such joy watching others receive rewards as well. Then, we will give them right back to God as a thank you for what He did for us. What a joyful sight that will be as we all celebrate the gift of salvation and a forever home with God!

Have I gotten off topic? I am sure you are still wondering about jobs in heaven. Will we work there, or not? I am leaning toward, yes. I think God will continue to allow us to use our gifts for His glory. I think He will continue to encourage us to work together for His kingdom. I think we will find joy in working for Him. What do you think?

 What if you had a job in heaven? What would it be? Draw a picture or write about it below.

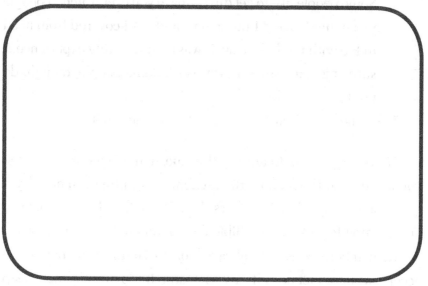

# 52

## Will You Get Dirty in Heaven?
## Do You Have to Take Showers?

I wanted to end with this question, because it was my favorite of all the questions my Sunday school friends asked. We touched on it at the beginning of this book, but let's think about it again now that we have learned all about heaven. How would you answer it now?

Here are some points that might help you as you wonder.

1. God has made us clean and spotless from sin.
2. Nature is full of dirt, and there is no reason to think we won't be surrounded by nature.
3. God has made heaven an awesome place for you.
4. Some people like to get dirty—have you ever watched people run in mud races? I ran in one, and I got covered from head to toe with mud and clay. It was an interesting experience. I sure enjoyed a shower afterward! Some people, though, do not like to get dirty!
5. Some people enjoy showers. My son does not!

However you would answer this question, I hope it has gotten you to stop and think about the excitement awaiting you one day. I hope you no longer have any fears about heaven, and I hope that you are learning to look in your Bible for answers to tough questions.

Remember, we should always look to God's Word before we accept what someone tells us as truth. Keep wondering. Keep dreaming. Keep asking God to reveal His truth to you. Go to church and ask tough questions. I guarantee your Sunday school teachers will be glad you did.

I want to leave you with thoughts from Hebrews 6.

It is impossible for God to lie. He has promised you a home with Him forever. He will never change his mind. He loves you. He has given you hope. In this world, where Satan wants to pull us away from Jesus, we are anchored to Jesus. Thanks to what He did for us on the cross, we will never lose Him or the salvation we've been given. Jesus is with God preparing a place for us. We will join Him there, and He will care for us forever. Because Jesus took the punishment we deserved, He became that sacrifice (the Lamb) for us. He also became our High Priest, ensuring we can approach the throne of God with confidence. There is no longer anything separating us from Him. Jesus never sinned. He took on our sins so that we could be set free from sin and could enter God's presence. Washed clean by the blood of Jesus, we can spend forever with our Creator. He is waiting for us and one day will say, "Well done my good and faithful servant."

I don't know about you, but I cannot wait for that glorious day!

God, You are Holy, Holy, Holy! You are Worthy and Mighty. Thank you for saving us. Thank you for loving us. Thank you that You keep your promises, and when Adam and Eve had to leave the Garden of Eden because of sin, You gave us all a way back to You. Help us to trust You with Your plans for us, and help us to look forward to our forever home with You. Give us boldness to share this truth with our friends and family so they might choose to love You and trust You too! In Jesus's precious name we pray, Amen!

# Author's Note

Thank you for reading this book! God has truly blessed me in the process of writing it. I hope it was a blessing to you as well, and that it encouraged you to grow your relationship with Jesus as you learned more about your forever home.

Parents, if you or your child enjoyed this book, would you mind leaving a review in any location where it is sold, or letting friends know about this resource for children? Your support is always appreciated and will allow me to continue to write more books—hopefully turning this into a series of "Kid Questions" books.

# About the Author

Lindsey Hilty was born and raised in Ohio and lives near Cincinnati with her husband and two children. Lindsey worked as a newspaper reporter for six years and then took on the roles of stay-at-home mom, home educator, and freelance writer. She has served in children's ministry for 20 years, and she especially enjoys teaching elementary-age students.

Printed in the United States
by Baker & Taylor Publisher Services